To my Parents, my Family
and Elspeth

The Architecture of the Halifax Piece Hall 1775 – 1779

Philip Smithies

On the cover: the courtyard of the Piece Hall, Halifax.

ISBN 0 9513935 0 2

Printed by Stott Brothers Limited, Halifax, England

Contents

FOREWORD

We take the Georgians too much for granted. So often it is confidently assumed that Georgian buildings are known, researched, admired, safe. This may be true of the country houses which receive so much, perhaps too much attention. But there is much more to the legacy of the 18th century: much of it less glamorous, more intriguing and still, often, at risk. And then there is something as extraordinary as the Halifax Piece Hall.

The Piece Hall ought to be one of the sights of England, but it is comparatively unknown. Perhaps that is because Halifax is not so much visited, both owing to the blinkered prejudice of southerners and the fastidious tastes of aesthetes who care only for the aristocratic and the rural. But even in the fine, dignified town of Halifax it is possible to miss the Piece Hall, for its spacious glory is a well kept secret. Coming upon it is like finding one of the great mosques of Delhi or Cairo; a vast sea of calm hidden in the midst of bustling, narrow streets.

I had assumed that the architectural history of something so remarkable must be fully investigated; then Philip Smithies came to me at the Architectural Association and told me that Who Designed the Piece Hall remained an open question. What had all our architectural historians been doing? Most student architectural theses are worthless and derivative. Mr Smithies' offering was different and a rare pleasure to read. It broke new ground and was a serious analysis of an unusual and fascinating monument. I am delighted that his researches are now made available in this book.

The history of the Piece Hall is not just of local interest as the building is a monument of national importance. It also adds so much to our understanding of the Georgian Age – of the process by which public buildings were decided upon, designed, raised and paid for; of the sort of men involved in such projects, their businesses and skills, their inspirations and aspirations. Above all, this history celebrates the central, illuminating phenomenon: the extraordinary fact that the wool merchants in a town in the West Riding of Yorkshire in the Reign of George III wished to conduct their business in an expensive structure which consciously emulated the grandeur of Imperial Rome.

Gavin Stamp

Preface and Acknowledgements

I should begin by saying that I am not a professional historian but a working architect. My study of the Piece Hall, I am sure, must suffer from some shortcomings but I hope any that may become apparent will be ascribed to my inexperience. In my research I have always tried to keep to the evidence and go wherever it appeared to lead. If it has not always been possible to arrive at a definite position, I have endeavoured to make it clear that doubt still persists and any conclusions that I might draw, are an interpretation only.

Often, because it seemed they had an important bearing on the Hall, I have outlined the work and thoughts of some of the greatest of European architects and theorists. These are very deep waters and in seeking to explain their significance as well as convey my view of their relationship to the Piece Hall, I have not hesitated to make full use of acknowledged authorities. Much the same is true for my discussions of unfamiliar social, economic and historical developments. Specifically I must thank Sir John Summerson for permitting me to make use of substantial quotations from his books, 'Georgian London' and 'The Classical Language of Architecture'.

Unfamiliar subjects have been a frequent difficulty; often where I thought I knew a little, I repeatedly found I knew nothing. My beginning was marked by this experience. Born and raised in Halifax, and from an early age desiring only to be an architect, it is shameful to confess that I had sauntered through the architectures of Athens and Rome before I ever set foot in the Piece Hall. I can only put this down to youth and the common failing of believing that what is near at hand is nothing to things far away. Happily, with the perspective of distance and time, my recompense is the appreciation that the Hall, in the extraordinary setting of Halifax, may not be in the front rank of Europe's, or indeed Britain's, finest buildings, but it is worthy of their company.

It was my father's suggestion that the Piece Hall should be the subject of my Architectural Association Diploma Thesis. After a delay of several years the Thesis was eventually completed in April 1987. The favourable way it was received encouraged me to believe that others might well be interested and so, after further research and some re-writing, I have published it in the form of this private book.

That I am able to do this is largely through the great effort of my father in typing and organising the whole of the text and the support of my mother. I am very grateful to both of them. I have, as well, to thank Jackie Burrell and Elspeth Young for their much appreciated typing of preliminary material and my supervisor, Gavin Stamp, for his help and advice in suggesting useful directions of research and for contributing his generous foreword. For assistance in proof-reading, but particularly for guidance and encouragment in the ways of publishing and support in the launch of the book, I would especially like to thank Alan Machin of the Calderdale Inheritance Project. I also very much appreciate the photography of Peter Hollings both for the excellence of his work and patience with the frequent revisions to my requirements.

Finally, I am grateful to all those who made available articles and information, particularly Howard Colvin, and to the many libraries and librarians, chiefly the Halifax Reference Library and the Royal Institute of British Architects, but also the Architectural Association Slide Library, the National Monuments and Records Library, and the libraries of Huddersfield, Leeds, Bradford and Wakefield all of whose kind assistance has been invaluable.

Halifax, July 1988.

Sources of Illustrations

Where not otherwise stated drawings and photographs are by, or in the possession of, the author.

PHOTOGRAPHS

Peter Hollings: **Covers, 3, 14, 15, 21, 27, 31, 32, 33, 34, 35, 36, 37, 38, 39.** The Halifax Courier: **5.** Leeds City Libraries: **24, 25.** Architectural Association: **40, 68, 75**; AA/Carlos Alvarez **43**; AA/Paul Simpson **44**; AA/Sir John Summerson **72**. National Monuments and Records Library: **73**. The British Architectural Library: **76**.

REPRODUCTIONS FROM BOOKS, PRINTS AND DOCUMENTS.

Calderdale Reference Library and Archive: Rev. Watson, *The History and Antiquities of Halifax*, 1775, **1, 86;** *Jacob's Directory of the Manufacturer's Hall in Halifax*, 1787, **2; 6, 7, 8;** *Jacob's History of Halifax*, 1789, **13,** ; George Walker, *Costume of Yorkshire* 1814, **26;** Bankfield Museum, Halifax, **12, 87.** Mr J. S. Roberts, **9.** The British Architectural Library: Facsimile of Filarete's *Treatise*, Florence early 1460's, **41;** L. B. Alberti, *Ten Books on Architecture (De Re Aedificatoria)* Trans. G. Leoni, London 1755, **45, 46;** Palladio, *Four Books of Architecture*, Trans. Isaac Ware, London 1738, **47, 48, 77;** William Chambers, *Treatise on Civil Architecture*, London 1759, **69;** Batty Langley *The City and Country Builder's and Workman's Treasury of Designs* ..., London 1740, **71, 74, 80, 81, 82;** William Pain, *The Builder's Companion and Workmen's General Assistant*, London 1762, **83, 84;** William Pain, *The Practical Builder, or Workman's General Assistant*, London 1774, **85;** J. N. L. Durand, *Précis des Leçons d'Architecture ... II*, Paris 1809, **79;** George Richardson, *The New Vitruvius Britannicus*, London 1802, **10, 11.** Raphael Custos, Engraving 1616, Staatliche Graphische Sammlung, Munich, **42.**

1 

2 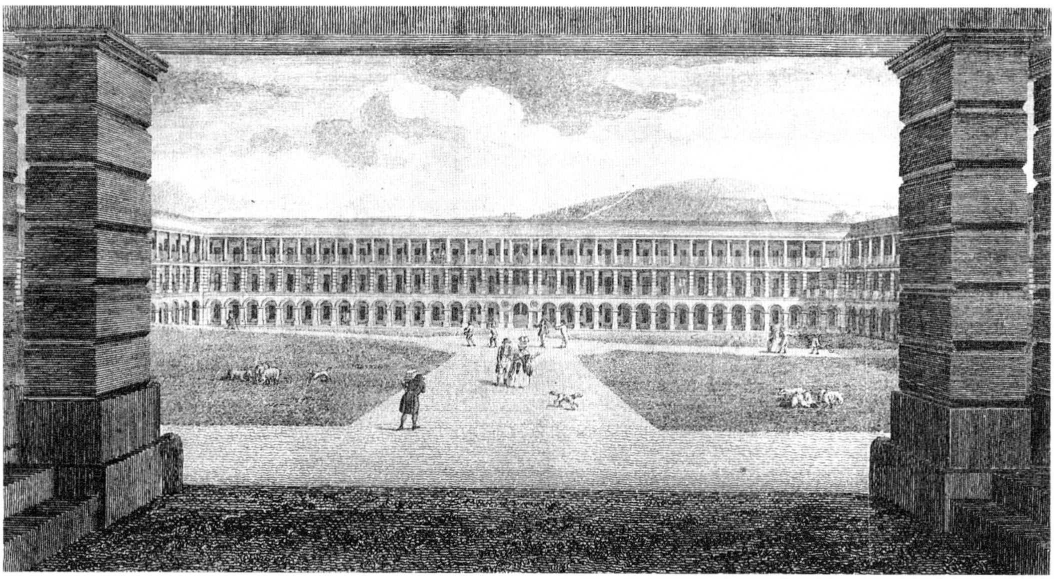

1 Halifax in the 1760's from the south-east prior to the building of the Piece Hall and the Independent Chapel.

2 Burgess' engraving of the Piece Hall courtyard from the West Gate, 1787. Note the repeated openings of door and window in the basement arcade; the arched openings we see today are not original.

INTRODUCTION

PIECE HALL, Thomas Street. Built as a cloth market in 1775 etc. by Thomas Bradley. Large open rectangle entered from the W by an archway with pediment and lantern over. The large area has two-storeyed colonnades all round, with square rusticated pillars below whose length decreases towards the E, and Tuscan columns above. The building has over 300 rooms and is the most noteworthy architectural monument of Halifax.

Nikolaus Pevsner, *Yorkshire The West Riding*, 1959.

From the time of its opening as a cloth market to its present use as a museum and monument the Piece Hall has never been the subject of detailed study and has remained, architecturally, a little known building. Halifax is not a town widely associated with outstanding architecture and should by chance a visit be made, it would be unremarkable if the Hall were missed altogether. This obscurity can perhaps be blamed on the peculiar nature of its form and the great changes that have taken place in its surroundings. Originally it stood in open fields, but the setting has been transformed by the enveloping *1*
expansion of the town during the 19th century, the demolition, in 1959, of the brick Georgian square which stood in front of it and the eventual replacement of this by a new shopping and car-park redevelopment in 1983.

The recent removal of buildings has uncovered more of the Hall to view, in particular the main entrance facade. Here, blank arcading flanks a grand Tuscan portico containing the low narrow entrance. *31*
Beyond lies the great concealed courtyard, 76 yards wide, 95 yards long, formed from three storeys of *2 32*
regular open galleries comprising a basement arcade, a middle gallery of rusticated piers and an upper *37*
colonnade of Tuscan columns. It is an extraordinary space and its discovery by each new visitor must be *36*
a complete and pleasing surprise, awakening great curiosity as to its origin, purpose and architecture.

The many articles written on the Hall have been chiefly by local historians and the earliest date from shortly after its opening in 1779, though the first detailed account was not published until 1887. Compiled by a local man, F. A. Leyland, this seems to have been based on original material, primarily the Minutes of the Piece Hall Committee, now lost to us. Subsequent articles rely largely on this. All are, for the most part, essentially social histories of the circumstances that gave rise to the Hall, its first use as a cloth market, then as a meeting place and finally as a fruit and vegetable market. They are very full accounts to which little can be added and provide a sound foundation from which any further study of the Hall must start. For this reason I have treated the Hall's past as briefly as is necessary to establish the historical background[1].

Since the ambition of these earlier writers went little beyond factual narration any thoughts they put forward to explain the nature and origin of the architecture were rather limited. The more recent articles of J. S. Roberts represent a significant advance from these in their specific concern with the architecture, particularly the question of the authorship of the Hall but also through their delineation of the way a more extensive study might best proceed. Derek Linstrum's subsequent regional survey 'West Yorkshire Architects and Architecture' did not, though, pursue research further but confined itself to what was already known.

The continuing lack of a full and proper explanation has left the splendour of the Hall a fascinating mystery which I have sought to unravel. I have begun by gathering and assessing the fragments of information contained in the disparate and unconnected articles and putting them together – like so many pieces of a jig-saw – to form a clear picture of what is assured fact and what is ambiguous.

1. See bibliography.

Naturally many pieces were missing and the assembly of some parts is derived more from reasoning than
certainty. However imperfect the picture, the connection of what had been previously separately known
disclosed a great deal. It also clearly revealed where knowledge was missing altogether and it is in these
areas that my efforts have been most concentrated. The building has been recorded in measured
drawings to enable a specific investigation of its origins and character. As far as is allowed by the shortage
of original documentary evidence, the inception and development of the Hall has been traced and the
authorship of the building settled. The understanding of the designers gained from this suggested where
to look for the likely general and detailed architectural sources for the building. Then the Piece Hall has
49 been set in a reconstruction of the plan of Halifax in 1779 which has revealed much of the size, location,
arrangement and articulation of the Hall which is otherwise obscure. To complete the background to the
building, it has been discussed in the general context of the cloth halls of the surrounding rival towns that
16 preceded and gave rise to it. Again, this was valuable as it became clear that the Piece Hall is a part, and
in many respects, a culmination of an architectural evolution which began in 1710 with the erection of
the Tammy Cloth Hall in Wakefield. It is not a building that appeared, so to speak, out of architectural
thin air.

In the same way a careful search has been made for the prototypes of the classical details, the
columns, the piers, the entrance gateway, the cornices and so forth in the builder's pattern books of the
18th century prior to 1775. Though, without original documents, it cannot be proved that these were
the actual models, the closeness of the detailing and proportions establishes a convincing case.
Similarly, the origins of the general architectural form of the Hall have been sought in English 18th
century architectural literature and as a result comparisons of the Piece Hall with two closely related
45 46 Italian Renaissance reconstructions of Roman 'Piazze' have been included. The first is from Alberti's
47 48 'Ten Books on Architecture' and the second from Palladio's 'Four Books of Architecture'; these I offer as
credible prototypes of the Hall. In addition to the resemblance in form, the Hall also seems to contain a
fragment of the proportional system embodied in both these 'Piazze'. The subtlety of this system and the
extent and meaning of its presence in the Hall is discussed at some length.

As a matter of pure speculation I have concluded with a few thoughts on the Piece Hall's relationship to English 18th century theory, the French neo-classical theory of Laugier and its place in the local development of 18th and 19th century industrial building. These reflections are not intended to be definitive; they are thoughts which to me seem appropriate in throwing some light on the intellectual framework by which the Hall is encompassed through the ambivalence of its adopted architectural form and place in time. The shortcomings of factual evidence leave open the possibilities of different interpretations on this and other aspects of the Hall. There is much room for further research, for instance the careers and works of the Hope brothers. But pre-eminent must be the discovery of the Minutes of the Piece Hall Committee last referred to in 1921. Study of these would be an immense gain and much that currently belongs to the sphere of argument would become simple fact. In their absence, though, I think my more comprehensive approach represents a significant improvement on the fragmented research carried out over the years. It will, I hope, be not only a detailed and informative guide to the casual admirer of the Hall, but also a helpful starting point for those who wish to explore further.

CHAPTER ONE

Cloth Manufacture and Organisation[1]

The Pennines of West Yorkshire lent themselves to the manufacture of cloth: sheep were reared on the hills and frequent rainfall provided a plentiful water supply to drive machinery and prepare the cloth. Cloth manufacture began towards the end of the 16th century as a means of supplementing the meagre incomes of farmers and the period of confiscation of monastic lands and the enclosure movements of the 16th and 17th centuries encouraged the tendency further. By the middle of the 18th century it had become a large cottage industry which provided the livelihood of the majority in the area and had brought great wealth to a fortunate few.

The process of manufacture began with the shearing of the sheep. The raw wool was first picked clean and then greased to protect it during the abrasive carding and spinning operation. Carding untangled the knotty mass of wool with special cards studded with iron pins which teased and fluffed out the fibres, stroking them into slivers. The fleecy slivers were then spun into yarn on the great wheel by women and children – as many as half a dozen spinsters might be needed to keep one weaver working full time. When farm work allowed, the men would weave the yarn prepared by their families. Warp yarn was put onto a beam and sized (covered in paste to protect it from shuttle damage). Weft yarn was wound round bobbins and the cloth woven on narrow wooden looms. The invention of the 'flying shuttle' in 1733 by Kay greatly reduced the strain and labour of weaving.

The woollen piece straight from the loom was a loose web of interwoven yarns. The process of fulling, which felted the fibres together so no single thread could be seen, made the cloth strong, warm and windproof. First the piece was soaked in stale urine ('lant') to speed up the felting process and then it was trampled underfoot, or hammered, in a trough of water to which 'Fullers Earth' had been added to cleanse the cloth of soap and oil. The sodden cloth, now slightly shrunk, was removed and hooked to a frame hung between tenterposts to fix the width and allow the cloth to dry. Once dry, the surface of the cloth was brushed up with teasels and the raised surface cropped with huge shears. The finished piece would be dyed and pressed and then it was ready for sale. At the time of the construction of the Piece Hall a cloth maker could prepare the yarn and weave a 'piece' of kersey (a coarse, narrow woollen cloth – one of many different types woven) in time for the weekly market.

Fulling mills were built by those who could afford it, or by a consortium of clothiers, and communities grew around them. Daniel Defoe in his 'A Tour Through the Whole Island of Great Britain', published between 1724 and 1725, vividly described this way of life in the West Riding at the start of the 18th Century.

> "... *after we had mounted the third hill, we found the country, in short, one continued village, though mountainous in every way, as before; hardly a house standing out of a speaking distance from another and (which soon told us their business) the day clearing up, and the sun shining, we could see that almost every house there was a tenter, and almost on every tenter a piece of cloth, or kersey, or shalloon, for they are the three articles of that country's labour* ... *Then, as every clothier must keep a horse, perhaps two, to fetch and carry for the use of his manufacture, to fetch home his wool and his provisions from the market, to carry his yarn to the spinners, his manufacture to the fulling, and when finished, to the market to be sold and the like; so every manufacturer keeps a cow or two, or more for his family, and this employs the two or three or four pieces of enclosed land about his house, for they scarce sow corn enough for their cocks and hens;* ... *Among the manufacturers' houses are likewise*

1. Many of the details of the evolution of the cloth industry in this chapter come from 'The Story of Old Halifax,' Chapter XIII, T. W. Hanson, 1920.

scattered an infinite number of cottages or small dwellings, in which dwell the workmen who are employed, the women and children of whom, are always busy carding, spinning etc., so that no hands being unemployed ... This is the reason we saw so few people without doors; but if we knocked at the door of any of the master manufacturers, we presently saw a houseful of lusty fellows, some at the dyefat, some dressing the cloths, some in the loom, some one thing, some another, all hard at work and full employed upon the manufacture and all seeming to have sufficient business ..."

Though Defoe painted a contented picture many starved when there was a bad harvest or wool was scarce. Famine and riots occurred in 1699 and 1728 through these disasters.

Defoe went on to describe the conduct of business by the merchants and clothiers at a central market in his report of the Leeds cloth market before the provision of a purpose built hall.

"Early in the morning, there are trestles placed in two rows in the street, sometimes two rows on a side, but always one row at least; then there are boards laid across these trestles, so that the boards lie like long counters on either side, from one end of the street to the other. The clothiers come early in the morning with their cloth; and as few bring more than one piece, the market being so frequent, they go into the inns and public houses with it, and there set it down.

At seven o'clock in the morning, the clothiers being supposed to be all come by that time, even in winter, the market bell rings; it would surprise a stranger to see in how few minutes, without hurry or noise, and not the least disorder, the whole market is filled; all the boards upon the trestles are covered with cloth, close to one another as the pieces can lie longways by one another, and behind every piece of cloth the clothier standing to sell it ... As soon as the bell has done ringing, the merchants and factors, and buyers of all sorts, come down, and coming along the spaces between the rows of boards, they walk up the rows and down as their occasions direct. Some of them have their foreign letters of orders with patterns sealed on them, in rows, in their hands and with those they match colours, holding them to the cloths as they think they agree to, when they see any cloths to their colours, or that suit their occasions, they reach over to the clothier and whisper, and, in the fewest words imaginable, the price is stated; one asks, the other bids, and 'tis agree, or not agree in a moment. The merchants and buyers generally walk up and down twice on each side of the rows, and in little more than an hour all the business is done; in less than half an hour you will perceive the cloths begin to move off, the clothier taking it up upon his shoulders to carry it to the merchants house; and by half an hour after eight o'clock the market bell rings again, immediately the buyers disappear, the cloth is all sold or if here and there a piece happens not to be bought, 'tis carried back to the inn, and, in quarter of an hour, there is not a piece of cloth to be seen in the market. Thus, you see, ten or twenty thousand pounds value in cloth, and sometimes much more, bought and sold in less than an hour, and the laws of the market the most strictly observed as any I ever saw done in any market in England ... By this quick return the clothiers are constantly supplied with money, their workmen are duly paid, and a prodigious sum circulates through the county every week."

The Halifax market must have closely resembled this before the Piece Hall was built both in the manner of business and wealth of the trade. There had been a specialised building in Halifax known as the Cloth and Linen Hall in the 17th century but by the beginning of the 18th century it was in poor repair and renovation was necessary. Trade grew and by the 1770's manufacturers were having to sell their cloth in the street, in the way described above at Leeds. Dissatisfaction with the weather and thieves aroused a desire for a Hall, big enough to contain all the manufacturers, and this led to the Piece Hall, built between 1774 and 1779. At Halifax the original subscribers paid £28 for a room; for the smaller weaver a charge was made to exhibit his goods on the grass in the courtyard. A Committee, elected from the manufacturers, administered the Hall.

The rules and hours for selling cloth were strict. The Hall opened for business only between 10 a.m. and 12 noon every Saturday. At 11.55 a.m. the closing bell started ringing and rang for five minutes.

At the end of that time, anyone caught selling or buying cloth was charged a fine of 5/-. From 8 a.m. until 9.45 a.m. and between 12.30 p.m. and 4 p.m. either a cart with one horse only, or pack horses were allowed into the square to deliver and take away goods. No activities other than the sale of woollen or worsted were allowed in the building. As manufacturers and buyers had to travel great distances to be in Halifax at a particular time and since business hours were so short, many stayed at regular inns where they could be contacted.

Due to the popularity of the Hall the North Gate was quickly found to be inadequate for the numbers hurrying to leave at the close of the market and so the West Gate was formed in 1782; in 1785 *33*
a porter's lodge was added outside the North Gate. Accommodation for all must have been insufficient as a line of manufacturers' 'shops' was gradually built, by others, along the approach road to the porter's lodge eventually cutting the northern elevation visually in half. These additions have long since gone and their appearance is unknown.

Though there were many independent small clothiers working and selling their cloth in the Piece Hall, the international success of the area came with men like Samuel Hill, a manufacturer and merchant of Soyland near Ripponden, Halifax, who employed many, perhaps hundreds, of cloth makers in his proto-industrial business. He worked direct to merchant's orders, from Britain and from abroad, and exported his cloth as far afield as Persia. Originally producing woollens, he turned to the new worsteds and draperies and was very successful. In 1747 his annual turnover was above £35,000 and much of his business had to be put out to others in the area.

The industrial system that evolved from Samuel Hill and others like him, paralleled the old cottage industry but grew in importance and strength as the century wore on. With hindsight, the clothiers days were numbered and, built towards the end of the clothier supremacy, the Hall has to take on something of the character of a swansong. But if it was such a peroration, then, the very richness of the Hall is eloquent proof that it was one far from apparent to its builders.

The Piece Hall was, however, initially successful and enjoyed a period of prosperous trading that lasted until the end of the 18th century. From then on the domination of the factory system became clear. New yarns were spun on mechanised spinning frames, in mills driven by water (and later steam) power and the region expanded and diversified into woollen broadcloth, worsted, cotton and fustian manufacturing. Merchants found it more convenient to visit the mechanised mills to buy or order what they required there. The clothier cottage industry nevertheless persisted beyond the 1850's producing specialised high quality cloth.

As trade declined, the strict rule that only woollen or worsted cloth should be traded in the Hall and no other activity permitted, had to be altered. After 1815 cotton goods were sold, the day of the market was changed from Saturday to Wednesday and the Hall was let for political meetings, religious reformers and even firework displays. But despite these efforts, by 1867 the Committee was aware that the Piece Hall was no longer a viable proposition and they approached the Halifax Corporation with the suggestion that it should be taken over as a gift which they did in 1868. In 1871 they converted it to a wholesale fish, fruit and vegetable market and the south gate was enlarged to allow vehicle access, the *34*
existing cast iron double gates replacing the old solid oak doors. Later, lean-to buildings were erected all round the perimeter of the courtyard and three brick structures placed in the centre. Doubtless it was the benign neglect of this conversion that made possible the Hall's survival through the ensuing century.

By 1971 the Piece Hall had become clearly unsuitable as a wholesale market and this business was dispersed to other places. After some discussion of the possible demolition of the Hall, thankfully, the Halifax Corporation instead took advantage of Government grants for restoration and in the process of renovation an industrial museum, art gallery, antique shops and cafe were added. The restored Hall was finally opened to the public on 3rd July 1976 in its last and most apposite role as an historic monument.

3

4

5

3 Stansfield, Lower Ashes, a clothier hill farm above Todmorden re-modelled with classical additions, about 1759. The rusticated gate posts are very similar to the rusticated piers of the Piece Hall.

4 Hope Hall, a good example of a formal classical house of the later 18th century.

5 One of the mansion blocks forming Caygill's Square before its demolition in 1959. It was, by accounts, a finer building than appears here. The garden of the Square lay in front of it to the right of the picture.

CHAPTER TWO

The Development of The Piece Hall Design

It would be misleading to assume that in 1774 Halifax was a backwater uncomplicated by any interest in architecture. Very little is known about the first Norman and Medieval buildings of the town but its later history records a substantial architectural tradition, the creation and evolution of which is, to a large extent, inextricably bound up with the achievements of the Clothiers and the success of the cloth trade[1]. As early as the 15th century the wealth of the woollen industry bore fruit in the third rebuilding of the Parish Church of St. John the Baptist in the late perpendicular style. After they had honoured the House of the Lord in this way, the Clothiers then seem to have turned their attention and subsequent prosperity largely into the improvement of their own dwellings. A particularly rich period came in the 17th century which produced many remarkable houses through renovation as well as new building. They are striking for their unself-conscious blend of classical, English Renaissance elements with Gothic details and vernacular form. Good examples survive.

In the 18th century the Clothiers continued to channel their ever-increasing wealth into domestic architecture but the improvements began to reflect the changes in style and consistency brought about by the greater knowledge of Italian classicism and the accurate dissemination of this made possible through the builders' pattern books of the time. It is the transition from gentrified farm to formal house.
Stansfield, Lower Ashes, above Todmorden, is a late instance of the former category, Hope Hall, in 3
Clare Road, Halifax, typical of the latter; both still exist. But the best examples are the work of no less an 4
architect than John Carr of York, famous for the Crescent at Buxton and Harewood House near Leeds. Outside Halifax we owe to him Pye Nest (demolished) and White Windows (1768) and within the town two developments (not, however, connected with the cloth trade), Somerset House in George Street
(1766) and, as we shall see, two terraces of brick houses around a 'square'. 5

In the last quarter of the 18th century a change of emphasis from a concern with purely private building to an awareness of public needs becomes apparent. We know that by 1775 Assembly Rooms had been built and Jacob's 'History of Halifax' 1789, recorded that a public subscription had been started for a new market place on the east side of Southgate (on land bought for that purpose by 'Sir Watts Horton') and also for a new Theatre on Horton's estate near to Ward's End (the design of this latter building being described as 'plain and convenient'). By 1793 Halifax could also boast the Public Baths in Lilly Lane and perhaps other works were envisaged or carried out. The design and building of the Piece Hall has to be seen as part of this nascent public-spirited desire for the enrichment of the town that was eventually to reach full flowering in the generous benefactions of the Victorians.

With the disappearance of the Piece Hall Committee Minutes the only original, surviving documents describing the period of design are the letters and official notices published in the 'Leeds Mercury' newspaper[2]. The correspondence reveals that, unsurprisingly, the manufacturers were hardworking clothiers more concerned with business than 'gentlemen architects' but who, as their history suggests, were also mindful that their hall should not merely be practical but by its quality do honour to their town as well. Their decisions were reached democratically at open meetings which is very fortunate since, as in any democratic body, there were differences of opinion and these, along with official notices, appeared in the 'Leeds Mercury' in the years 1774 and 1775 in efforts to sway the manufacturers' decisions and in so doing allow the development of the design to be traced.

The first notice appeared in the 'Leeds Mercury' on Tuesday April 5th 1774 and explained that at the Halifax cloth market a meeting of manufacturers had popularly decided that a purpose-built hall

1. 'The Story of Old Halifax', T. W. Hanson, 1920.
2. Huddersfield Reference Library.

would be a much better place to sell cloth than in the street. Subsequent notices stated that any manufacturer who subscribed could join the association formed to build the Hall and a great number quickly did so. The merchants did not form part of the association but were invited to the meetings as interested parties. A notice, published on 19th April 1774, invited those who wished to sell land for the proposed Hall, to attend a meeting at which the manufacturers would choose which site they preferred. They also elected a committee to be responsible for the building of the Hall.

At this point an address was published in the 'Leeds Mercury', on May 10th 1774, encouraging the manufacturers to have ambitions for their Hall beyond mere utility:

> *"The present call is loud for ours; from our declining trade, from our immediate selves, and as connected with the interests of posterity, and the general good of the community . . . Nor let us be sparing of our subscriptions, for the honour of our County, and the welfare of rising periods. In a word let each endeavour to be employed to strike an unison with public utility: So shall future ages feelingly bless the present generation and neighbouring enemy fall at our feet."*

The same address, signed anonymously, 'A Manufacturer', also makes clear that disagreement had arisen over the siting of the Hall in the town:

> *"Let us not quarrel in regard to situation: the bee will find its cell, tho' in the desert: so the Merchants and Manufacturers, tho' detached from the accustomed seat of Business."*

In other words the Hall would work in any location. This apparent lack of appreciation of the possibilities of the architectural relationship between the largest and most important building in the town and the rest of Halifax was not shared by all.

Several sites were made available to the manufacturers. The one finally chosen came as the gift of John Caygill, a man of some standing in the town. Caygill was one of the most important figures in the creation of the Piece Hall. Born in Halifax in 1708, he was a wealthy man who owned the Talbot Inn, venue of all the Piece Hall meetings, and the Talbot Croft field to the south of Halifax. He was an imaginative developer of his property, to both his and the town's advantage, and it was his efforts that gave Halifax its most notable urban space.

There is uncertainty, but probably between the years 1759 and 1770, he speculatively built
49 mansions on the eastern and northern sides of his Talbot Croft, reputedly to the designs of John Carr of
5 York. They were large brick houses, arranged on two sides of a square around a communal garden. Entry to the square was through large double gates on the lower, eastern side. The western side of the square was formed by warehouses and Assembly Rooms; the Talbot Inn stood at the north-western corner. Inside, the houses were well appointed with handsome fireplaces, decorated ceilings and cornices in the principal rooms[3].

This was a unique development, the only example, as far as I am aware, of a square in Halifax. Perhaps it was planned in imitation of London squares. If this was so, it was a little ambitious to call it a square at all since it was far from being a replica of London architecture. Nevertheless, it was the only instance of thoughtful planning in a town of otherwise random expansion and it was the first use of brick in an area where it was far easier to use the local plentiful sandstone. The only part of Caygill's plan that came to nothing was a marble statue of himself, that was to have stood in the centre of the Square[4].

38 In 1772 'Square' Independent Chapel was built on (or beside) the Talbot Croft, but at a distance from the Square, by a disaffected Wesleyan, Titus Knight[5]. Like the mansions, it was constructed of brick with a classical Georgian vocabulary of stone Palladian windows and doors. Inside was a large galleried space with a fine plaster ceiling .

3. See 'The Square and the Piece Hall, Halifax', R. Bretton, Transactions of the Halifax Antiquarian Society, 1961.
4. The houses forming Caygill's Square were demolished in 1959 and the 'Square' Independent Chapel has been boarded up for some years.
5. The Halifax Evening Courier, 6th October 1979.

'Caygill's Square', as it became known, lacked a southern side and perhaps he wanted the intended Manufacturers' Hall as a building of sufficient size and quality to complete it. Whatever the truth of the matter, he wanted it so badly he was prepared to give valuable land away to the Manufacturers for the Hall to be built in that position – with the proviso that the Hall was completed by the end of 1778.

Only one other site was seriously considered by the manufacturers, a field known as the 'Cross Close' which lay on the northern side of the town. The only description of it comes from Ling Roth's 'Yorkshire Coiners' and he suggests that the site was confined and sufficient access was impossible; it appears on Moore's 1797 plan of Halifax. *49 87*

Nevertheless, a vote of subscribing manufacturers found 105 for the Talbot Croft and as many as 81 for the Cross Close. Feelings were strong enough for the defeated minority to break away, temporarily, to organise the building of a rival Hall on their preferred site. Notices from them appeared in the 'Leeds Mercury' well into June but nothing came of their efforts. This may have been because of the Merchants, who through letters in the 'Leeds Mercury' of May and June, urged the manufacturers to stay united saying they were 'determined to buy their goods there' (the Talbot Croft).

The chief reason for the choice of the Talbot Croft site must have been its being offered free, but there may also have been the secondary reason, deriving from an anonymous letter published in the 'Leeds Mercury' on May 27th 1774, which gave the manufacturers the following advice:

> *"Let no man impose upon you in this matter – Look with your own eyes – Judge for yourselves – See you have a large and open situation – The building clear to every view, and clear roads to at least three sides of it – Have full assurance for this – Trust no man's word, but see the obligations – Open air and much of it, will be found quite necessary for preserving your goods and doing business with pleasure – Be not concerned about this or that end of the town – where you fix your Hall, there will be the head – Nothing is of consequence to you but the navigation – To the town it will grow – strive not against this – Take care you fix it on the South; High or low is not material; Situations being equally advantageous."*

The important point here is the advice to place the building on the south of the town to take advantage of the 'navigation', a clear reference to the Calder and Hebble Canal which lay to the south of the town. The above letter, signed 'Aristides', almost certainly came from the Halifax Union Club who were great promoters of the Calder and Hebble Navigation[6]. Certainly the Piece Hall was built on the southern side of the town and had a southern gateway, but in the event, little traffic came from that direction. *34*

The Piece Hall Committee ignored the breakaway manufacturers and pressed on. In a notice, dated Halifax May 20th 1774 and published in the 'Leeds Mercury' on June 14th, the Committee announced that they would employ 'Proper Persons' to make plans for the purpose and that on the 25th June – only one month later – a meeting would be held for the manufacturers to decide which of the schemes to build. There is no record of the result of this meeting but the notice that appeared in the 'Leeds Mercury', dated Halifax August 3rd 1774, was addressed to Masons asking them to come and see the chosen design at the Talbot Inn from September 3rd onwards, in order that they might submit their proposals to the Committee the following week on the 10th September.

However there followed a delay of some months which, we can surmise from the following letter, dated 20th December 1774, was caused by a disagreement over two designs. This letter is important as the only description of an alternative Hall, and the only record and indication of the influences at work on the manufacturers and their thoughts.

"TO THE MANUFACTURERS AND SUBSCRIBERS OF THE INTENDED PIECE HALL, IN HALIFAX.

You have a plan of your intended Piece Hall, made by a native of this town which has undergone

6. In 1756 the Halifax Union Club decided to seek an Act of Parliament to make navigable the Calder River from Wakefield to Elland and so on to Halifax. One purpose in mind was to improve the transport of raw wool to the Halifax manufacturing area.

much inspection, and has I believe, your approbation before all others yet inspected. If it is put into execution it will be useful elegant and plain; and I apprehend may be finished with the money subscribed provided you employ no more of the gentlemen-architects; if you do consider to employ them, I fear too much of your subscriptions will be spent before you have adequate work done; and I may safely prophecy, before the whole be completed, you will have to subscribe afresh. The confusion and inconvenience that a circumstance of this sort would occasion, is obvious to any man of commonsense. I am informed that you have a Plan sent for a Circular Building, which, if put into execution will be attended with the following disadvantages, viz:

1. *a circular building will lose about one fifth of the ground so generously given;*
2. *a circular building to decline as the ground does, will have no right lines: every window, door, and course of masonry must consequently be attended with more expense;*
3. *the passages betwixt the shops will always run down or up-hill; and the fall of the ground, exceeding two inches per yard, part of the shops of 9 feet broad must be higher on one side than the other, by 6 inches or more. All the shops will have their proportionate decline;*
4. *no light can be had in a right line in these circular passages; therefore they are supposed to be lighted over doors, and all that can be obtained in that way may well be deficient;*
5. *the wood-work will be attended with more expense;*
6. *the roof will not have an equal bearing; and it cannot be done at so easy an expense as the roof of a square building. With regard to its appearance it will be rendered disagreeable by its considerable declension parallel to the ground; it will have a barren uniformity, and be totally destitute of that elegant simplicity which should adorn the manufacturers' Hall.*

All that I have further to add is to advise you to compare the Plans, and judge with impartiality. When you have seriously entered into the merits of them, I do not doubt you will agree with me in giving preference to that of your own townsman.

I am, Gentlemen, Yours etc. A Manufacturer."

17 18 The description of the circular building is very like the elliptical Cloth Hall opened in Huddersfield in 1766. Unfortunately the writer does not provide a similarly specific description of the design 'by a native of this town' which he preferred; he does, though, state that the roof of a circular building would not be done 'as easy an expense as the roof on a square building' which suggests that the other had a rectangular form. The disadvantage of a circular building losing one fifth of the ground is interesting in the light of what was eventually built since, ironically, the Piece Hall left a strip of the site 9 yards wide by 110 yards long, or roughly one tenth of the whole, untouched.

This persuasive letter was followed by a notice which appeared in the 'Leeds Mercury', dated January 25th 1775, announcing that 'a considerable number of subscribers' had seen a plan for their Hall which they approved and sought a meeting to consider their favoured design. An account by Maurice Garside[7], cites the 'Minutes of the Halifax Piece Hall Commmittee' as the source for his description of this subscriber's meeting so the following quotation has, I think, to be taken as an authentic record:

"The desired meeting was held on the 11th of February 1775 and it was then that Mr. Bradley's design for the Hall was unanimously agreed upon. In the April of the same year it was made known to masons and others, that persons willing to undertake the building of one fourth part of the intended Piece Hall in Halifax – the whole being designed to be let – might see the plans and specifications on application to the clerk, Mr. Simpson (who incidentally was clerk to the Calder and Hebble Navigation Company, of which Mr. Thomas Bradley was to become the chief engineer), to whom they were requested to send their proposals, on or before, the 11th of May 1775 when the Committee would attend at nine of the clock in the forenoon, to let the works."

7. Halifax Antiquarian Society Transactions, 1921 – 'The Halifax Piece Hall'. In a footnote Garside thanked the Right Honourable J. H. Whitley M.P. for allowing him to use the 'Minutes of the Piece Hall Committee' which formed the basis of his paper.

There are a number of points here. Firstly, that Thomas Bradley and his design are unequivocally given as the Piece Hall architect and the chosen project. Secondly, the invitation to masons to tender for one fourth part of the Hall 'that the Committee had decided to build', indicates a rectangular design. This perhaps refers to the design of a 'native of this town' advocated in the Manufacturer's letter. And thirdly, that the one month allowed for masons to make their estimates and tenders left little time and no brief to alter Bradley's design.

However, before we proceed to the events that followed, we must consider the earlier report of the above meeting written by the local historian, F. A. Leyland, in the 'Halifax Guardian' on May 7th 1887.

> *"The desired meeting was held on the 11th of February 1775, and it was then that Mr. Bradley's design for the Hall was unanimously agreed upon. In the April of the same year it was made known to the masons and others, that persons willing to undertake the building of one-fourth part of the intended Piece Hall, in Halifax – the whole being designed to be let – might see the plans and specifications on application to the clerk, Mr. Simpson, to whom they were requested to send their proposals on or before the 11th of May 1775, when the Committee would attend at nine of the clock in the forenoon, to let the works."*

Clearly, there is little difference between Leyland and Garside. There are various ways of explaining such similarity. Either Garside has plagiarized Leyland or, since Garside had acknowledged the Minutes of the Piece Hall Committee as the basis of his paper, Leyland, presumably, relied on the same source – both explanations seem likely. Writing a hundred years after the opening of the Piece Hall, and with no previous detailed articles to make use of, what source other than the 'Minutes' could have given rise to Leyland's long and specific account? If this is, indeed, what happened, then Leyland, would become an equally authentic record. Later, we shall see how Garside and Leyland agree in other important respects – even down to offering the same opinions.

The continuation of Leyland's article provides a nugget of information not found in Garside, or any other account or document, and goes to the heart of the dispute about who designed the Hall and who built it – apparently making the latter part of this argument quite plain.

> *"The erection of the Hall was let to the successful competitors, Messrs. Samuel and John Hope, contractors and builders, on the day before stated."* (That is, 11th May 1775.)

But however clear this seems to be, there are other sides of the question to consider, the first of which concerns two surviving documents which, it is reasonable to suppose, were made in response to the Committee's call to masons. The first[8], corresponding to the request for tenders for 'one fourth part' of the Hall, are 'Articles of Agreement' dated 10th June 1775 drawn up between the Committee and the *6*
following masons:

> *"... James Wood, William Ackroyd and John Preston all of Halifax, masons of the one part and James Pitchforth of Elland, mason and George Anderson of Guiseley, mason of the other part ... will do perform and execute all the mason's work for the South Quarter of the Piece Hall intended to be forthwith erected in the Talbot Field in Halifax At and for the prices and upon the Terms and Conditions stipulated – mentioned in the paper writing hereunto annexed And shall and will execute and finish all such masons work in a workmanlike manner and to the satisfaction of the Architect and Surveyor now appointed or hereafter to be appointed to superintend the building of the said Piece Hall the whole of which work to be finished and compleated within the time said James Pitchforth and George Anderson are by their Agreement with the Committee of the Subscribers towards erecting the said Piece Hall obliged to finish and complete the same And the same to be certified for by the said Architect and Surveyor."*

The 'annexed paper writing' scheduled the works the masons had contracted for. Only one page of this 7

8. Halifax Reference Library, MISC.3/72/1/2. See Appendix 1.

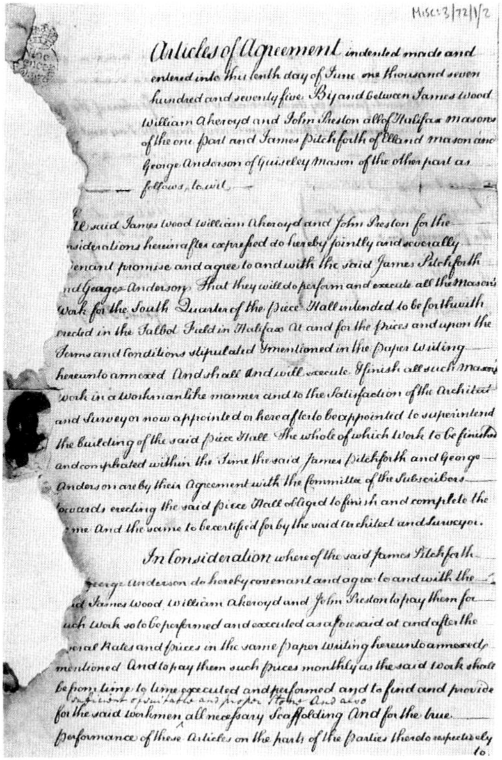
MISC 3/72/1/2

Articles of Agreement indented made and entered into this tenth day of June one thousand seven hundred and seventy five By and between James Wood William Akeroyd and John Preston all of Halifax masons of the one part and James Pitchforth of Elland mason and George Anderson of Guiseley Mason of the other part as follows, to wit —

The said James Wood William Akeroyd and John Preston for the considerations hereinafter expressed do hereby jointly and severally covenant promise and agree to and with the said James Pitchforth and George Anderson That they will do perform and execute all the Mason's Work for the South Quarter of the Piece Hall intended to be forthwith erected in the Talbot Field in Halifax At and for the prices and upon the Terms and Conditions stipulated & mentioned in the Paper Writing hereunto annexed And shall and will execute & finish all such Masons Work in a Workmanlike manner and to the Satisfaction of the Architect and Surveyor now appointed or hereafter to be appointed to superintend the building of the said Piece Hall The whole of which Work to be finished and compleated within the Time the said James Pitchforth and George Anderson are by their Agreement with the Committee of the Subscribers towards erecting the said Piece Hall obliged to finish and complete the same And the same to be certified for by the said Architect and Surveyor.

In Consideration whereof the said James Pitchforth George Anderson do hereby covenant and agree to and with the said James Wood William Akeroyd and John Preston to pay them for such Work so to be performed and executed as aforesaid at and after the several Rates and prices in the same paper Writing hereunto annexed mentioned And to pay them such prices monthly as the said Work shall be from time to time executed and performed and to find and provide sufficient of suitable and proper Stone And also for the said workmen all necessary Scaffolding And for the true performance of these Articles on the parts of the Parties thereto respectively to

6

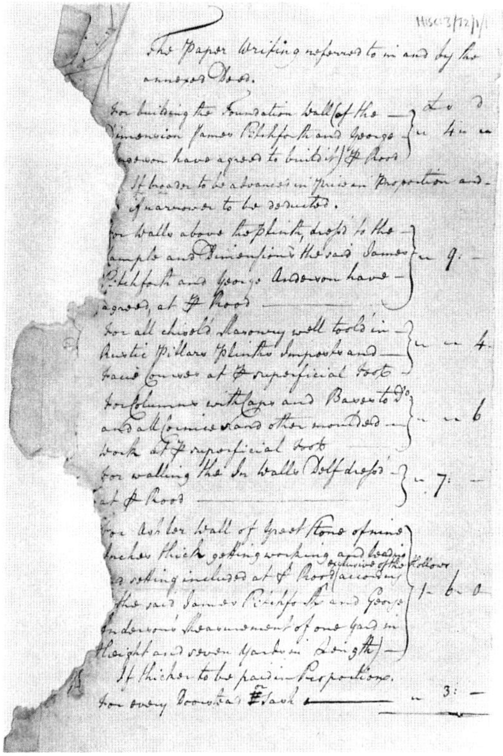
MISC 3/72/1/1

The Paper Writing referred to in and by the annexed Deed.

For building the Foundation Wall of the Dimension James Pitchforth and George Anderson have agreed to build it @ Rood — £ s d — 4 —

If broader to be advanced in Price in Proportion and if narrower to be deducted.

For Walls above the plinth, drops to the sample and Dimensions the said James Pitchforth and George Anderson have agreed, at @ Rood — 9 —

For all chisel'd Masonry well tool'd in Rustic Pillars Plinths Imposts and Band Courses at @ superficial foot — 4

For Columns with Caps and Bases to do and all Cornices and other moulded work at @ superficial foot — 6

For walling the In Walls Delf drops at @ Rood — 7 —

For Ashler Wall of great Stone of nine Inches thick getting working and leading exclusive of the Hollow ... being included at @ Rood according the said James Pitchforth and George Anderson's Measurement of one Yard in Height and seven Yards in Length — 1 6 0

If thicker to be paid in Proportion.

For every Doorstead @ each — 3 —

7

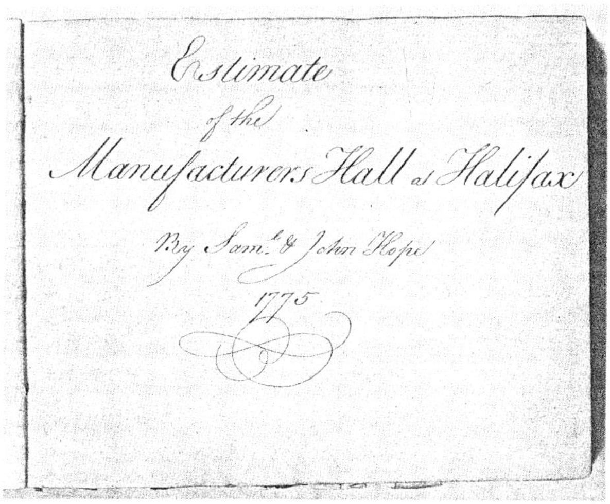
Estimate of the Manufacturers Hall at Halifax By Saml. & John Hope 1775

8

6 The Articles of Agreement between the Piece Hall Committee and contracting masons, 10th June 1775.

7 The schedule of works attached to the Articles of Agreement.

8 The title page of Samuel and John Hope's 'Estimate' 1775.

remains but it seems to correspond to the south side as built; for example, it lists the requirement for Rusticated piers.

The second document is a complete masons estimate. The 'Estimate of the Manufacturers' Hall at 8
Halifax' was signed by a Samuel and John Hope and dated 1775[9]. It is divided into four parts for the North, East, West and South sides of the Hall – which conforms to the Committee's decision for the tender to be in quarters. This estimate included almost all the items in the building and corresponds to the Piece Hall as originally built. The North side cost £1,950 17s 8d. The South side opposite was only marginally less at £1,923 12s 11¼d – a difference of only £27 4s 8¾d – despite the greater expense of the Tuscan gateway and the blank arcading that distinguished the north side. The west side, which had only two storeys, was the cheapest at £1,770 9s 2¼d. The east side with three full storeys was, as we would expect, the costliest at £2,815 18s 11½d.

Since, at this moment, the Piece Hall correspondence in the 'Leeds Mercury' ceased, the date of the commencement of construction and the details of what happened during building are not known. Unfortunately, both Leyland and Garside, are also silent on this period, which is a great loss. Consequently, despite Leyland's clear statement that the works were let to Samuel and John Hope, the Articles of Agreement leave a measure of ambiguity and we cannot be absolutely certain of the arrangements made for the erection of the Hall. The implication of the masons contract must be that the works were let in quarters to different contracting masons. From Leyland, we can infer that the Hopes were appointed as a kind of general contractor or builder, in which case the masons were most probably subcontractors working either under them or within their direction.

This interpretation is very neat and, I think, the most reasonable. The one part it leaves unexplained, the identities of the Architect and Surveyor appointed to superintend the works, will, I hope, become clearer in the more detailed discussion of the authorship of the Hall in the following chapter. Further information comes largely from Leyland's account, but refers only to the years after the opening of the Hall. At a meeting of the Committee, held on the 29th July 1780, it was ascertained that there had been paid up to that date £7,697 14s 8½d for the works, and afterwards, from 1782 to the 7th February 1785, with further works the final cost of erecting the Manufacturers Hall at Halifax is calculated to have been £9,692 00s 11½d[10]. The work on the Hall after the opening on 1st January 1779, was relatively small. Besides the creation of the West Gate and the porter's lodge, the only other
significant alteration was the addition over the new gate, in 1785, of a domed bellcote with a gilded 33
weather-vane in the form of a golden fleece. It is very similar to those on other cloth halls in the surrounding towns.

Messrs. J. & R. Swaine, the treasurers, wrote with details of the Piece Hall account to Mr Ralph of Halifax, Chairman of the Piece Hall Committee. The rooms were valued at £28. 4s. 0d.; there were 60 in the arcade, 126 in the Rustic gallery and 129 in the colonnade, 315 in all. The value of each room constituted the subscription of the manufacturer (some of which remained unpaid). The sum raised by these sales, every room being disposed of, was £8,883. From the letter it appears that the opposition to the Talbot Croft site was finally overcome by a donation of £840 from Caygill on the condition that the Hall should be built at that place; this was added to the amount realised by the sale of the rooms.

9. Halifax Reference Library, MISC.2/39/1. See Appendix 2.
10. It has been stated, however, that the entire amount expended on the structure was £12,000; perhaps the difference included the architect's fee and materials not mentioned in the particular estimates given above (F. A. Leyland, 'The Halifax Guardian', May 7th 1887).

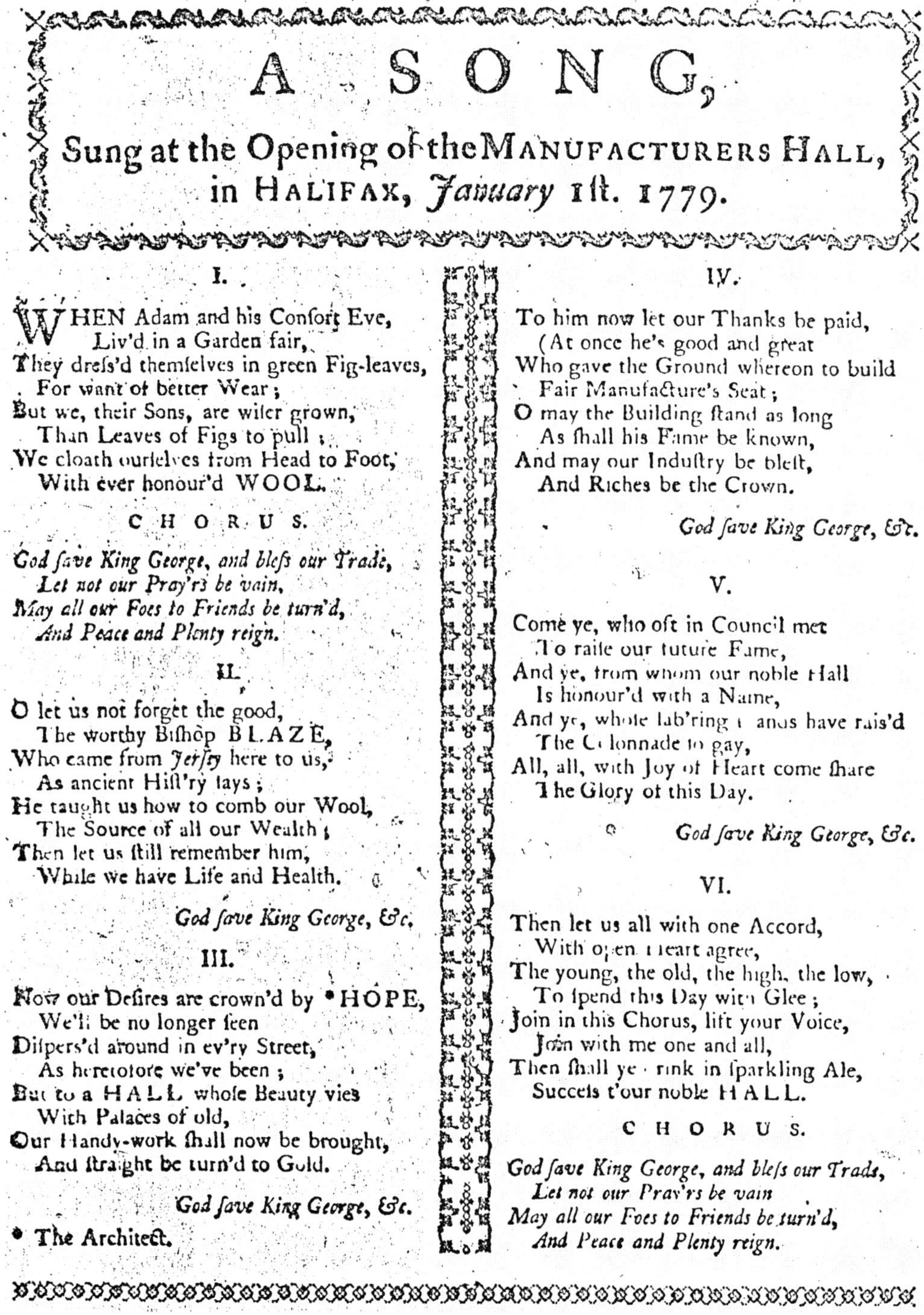

A SONG,

Sung at the Opening of the MANUFACTURERS HALL, in HALIFAX, *January* 1ſt. 1779.

I.

WHEN Adam and his Conſort Eve,
Liv'd in a Garden fair,
They dreſs'd themſelves in green Fig-leaves,
For want of better Wear;
But we, their Sons, are wiſer grown,
Than Leaves of Figs to pull;
We cloath ourſelves from Head to Foot,
With ever honour'd WOOL.

CHORUS.

God ſave King George, and bleſs our Trade,
Let not our Pray'rs be vain,
May all our Foes to Friends be turn'd,
And Peace and Plenty reign.

II.

O let us not forget the good,
The worthy Biſhop BLAZE,
Who came from *Jerſey* here to us,
As ancient Hiſt'ry ſays;
He taught us how to comb our Wool,
The Source of all our Wealth;
Then let us ſtill remember him,
While we have Life and Health.

God ſave King George, &c.

III.

Now our Deſires are crown'd by *HOPE,
We'll be no longer ſeen
Diſpers'd around in ev'ry Street,
As heretofore we've been;
But to a HALL whoſe Beauty vies
With Palaces of old,
Our Handy-work ſhall now be brought,
And ſtraight be turn'd to Gold.

God ſave King George, &c.

* The Architect.

IV.

To him now let our Thanks be paid,
(At once he's good and great
Who gave the Ground whereon to build
Fair Manufacture's Seat;
O may the Building ſtand as long
As ſhall his Fame be known,
And may our Induſtry be bleſt,
And Riches be the Crown.

God ſave King George, &c.

V.

Come ye, who oft in Council met
To raiſe our future Fame,
And ye, from whom our noble Hall
Is honour'd with a Name,
And ye, whoſe lab'ring Hands have rais'd
The Colonnade ſo gay,
All, all, with Joy of Heart come ſhare
The Glory of this Day.

God ſave King George, &c.

VI.

Then let us all with one Accord,
With open Heart agree,
The young, the old, the high, the low,
To ſpend this Day with Glee;
Join in this Chorus, lift your Voice,
Join with me one and all,
Then ſhall ye drink in ſparkling Ale,
Succeſs t'our noble HALL.

CHORUS.

God ſave King George, and bleſs our Trade,
Let not our Pray'rs be vain
May all our Foes to Friends be turn'd,
And Peace and Plenty reign.

9 The Piece Hall song sheet. Note the third verse referring to HOPE as the architect.

CHAPTER THREE

Who was the Architect of The Piece Hall?

If the economic origins of the Hall are clear and the development of the design known at least in outline, who then was actually responsible for its design? Mention has already been made of three men, Thomas Bradley and the brothers Samuel and John Hope. Though the earliest descriptions, such as 'Jacob's History of Halifax' 1789, credit no-one, ever since the publication of the 1837 edition of White's 'West Riding Directory', Thomas Bradley has always been considered the architect. The first substantial article to confirm Bradley's responsibility did not appear until 50 years later when F. A. Leyland wrote in the 'Halifax Courier' on April 9th 1887[1]:

> *"And fortunately, to design the colossal and magnificent structure they contemplated, there resided in the town, of which he was a native, Mr. Thos. Bradley, a gentleman, whose great architectural knowledge and ability combined with his correct classical judgement, enabled him to carry out, with grandeur, the imposing work which was entrusted to him."*

Later accounts by local historians all agree that Bradley was the architect with no suggestion that it might have been anybody else. But in 1978 another local historian, J. S. Roberts, argued that Bradley was not the architect at all but, that in fact, there were two other 'architects', the brothers Samuel and John Hope. Though Leyland's articles had specifically acknowledged their contribution as contractors and builders, he never referred to them as architects. Subsequently in the 1900's their signed 'Estimate for the Piece Hall' came into the possession of the local Antiquarian Society and an article, by an antiquarian using this Estimate, had been written in 1905, comparing the cost to build the Hall in 1775 with what it would have cost at the time of his writing, but he also declined to refer to them as the architects. Roberts' argument derives from the song composed for the Hall's inauguration on January 1st
1779, and in particular on a song sheet which he records as an original printed for the occasion. Verse III 9
begins:

> *"Now our Desires are crown'd by HOPE*"*

The asterisked HOPE is explained at the foot of the sheet as 'The Architect'. Roberts writes:

> *"The first line of the third verse makes the meaning of 'Hope' quite clear, except that the asterisk refers to 'The Architect' and not as we should reasonably expect 'The Architects'."*[2]

Roberts cites other buildings by the Hopes; this information comes, I think, from Colvin's 'Biographical Dictionary'. He concludes emphatically:

> *"There is little more I know about them except that there is no doubt whatever that they designed Halifax Piece Hall, one of Britain's outstanding buildings of the 18th century."*

However, I think Roberts dismisses Bradley too easily in this article and asserts the claims of the Hopes more strongly than is justified by the songsheet alone. Nevertheless, as no other evidence suggests

1. This account is the first half of two articles. The second, published in the 'Halifax Guardian' on May 7th 1887, we have already come across. For the reasons discussed in Chapter Two, I think it is reasonable to assume that both articles are sincere reports of the Piece Hall Committee Minutes.
2. 'The Halifax Piece Hall', 'The Yorkshire Architect' No. 58 Jan/Feb 1978. However, I think there is reason to doubt that this song sheet is one original to the Hall's opening since its title 'A SONG **Sung** at the opening of the MANUFACTURERS HALL' is in the past tense. This would be an odd way to introduce a song which had yet to be performed. Perhaps this sheet was printed after the event? The song had been first reproduced in Ling Roth's 'Yorkhire Coiners' 1906, but without the asterisked reference to the architect.

10

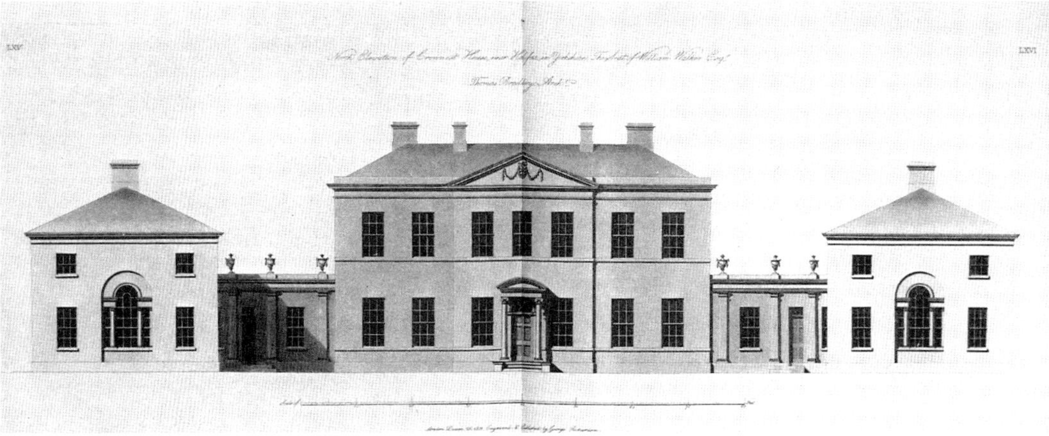

11

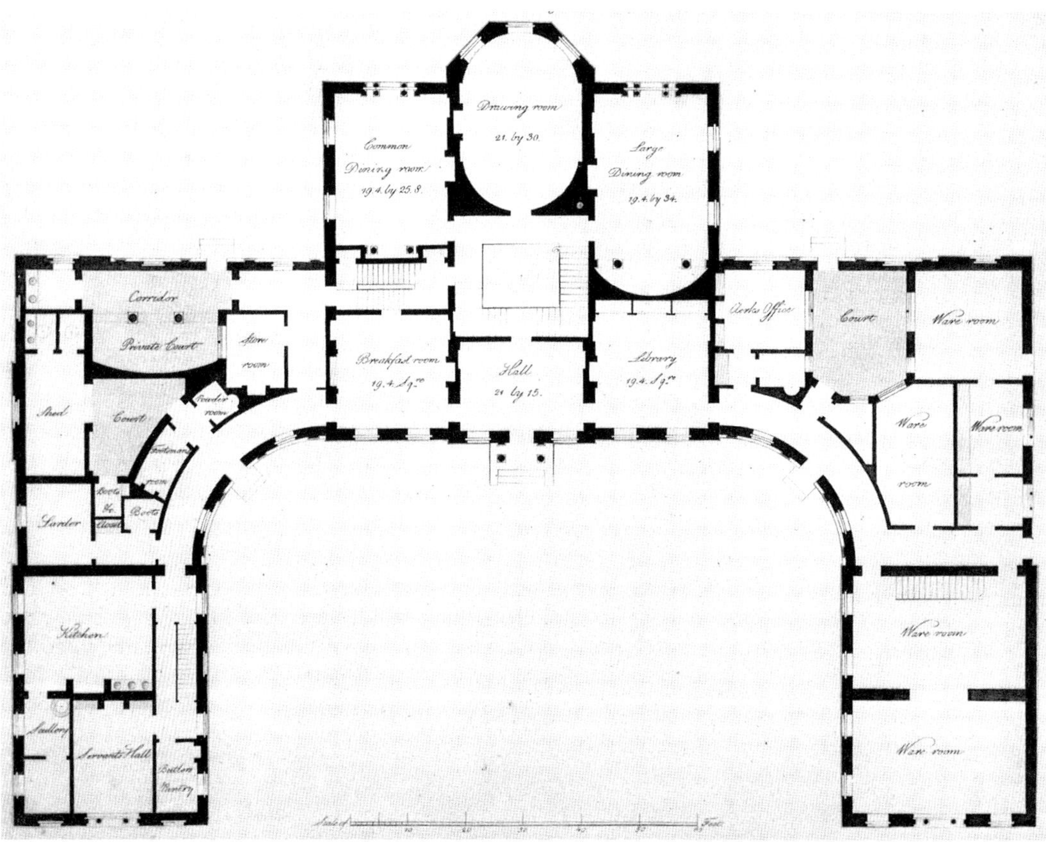

10 The elevation of the wool merchant William Walker's house, Crownest, 1788, designed by Thomas Bradley and published in Richardson's 'New Vitruvius Britannicus', 1802.

11 The plan of Crownest.

further candidates, the truth would appear to lie somewhere with these three.

As Thomas Bradley has the prior claim it seems best to start with him and the articles in which he appears as the architect. These accounts, beginning with Leyland's articles of 1887 and leading on to Garside's of 1921, are strikingly similar in what they say, making it, as we have seen, difficult to escape the conclusion that the Minutes of the Piece Hall Committee were the common basis for both. Garside wrote:

> *"From an Architectural point of view the Hall is particularly interesting. Mr. Thomas Bradley, the local architect entrusted with the fashioning of the plans of the Hall, advised that the edifice should not only be of colossal proportions so as to be well adapted for the primary use to which it was devoted but also that it should conform in design with the principles of Roman Classical Architecture as adapted to more modern circumstances by the greatest artists of the Italian Renaissance."*[3]

If Garside is accurately reporting the Minutes here – and there is no reason to doubt him – then Bradley, the local man, cannot be discounted despite what we know of the 'Hope' of the songsheet. However, it is the only evidence of Bradley's involvement, as all other references to him as the architect in other papers are unverified.

Further support for Bradley's claim can be derived from the public notices and letters published in the 'Leeds Mercury'. As we have seen the notices fell into two stages: the first included the commissioning of the plans, the public discussion of them and the selection of the preferred scheme; in the second stage came the calling of masons to tender and the letting of contracts. Only two designs are known in the first stage – one by a native of Halifax, 'useful, elegant and plain', and the other, by 'gentlemen architects', circular. At this stage the Hopes can be ruled out as designers because, as will become clear, they were neither natives of Halifax nor gentlemen architects. Since the circular design was obviously not chosen the most plausible interpretation that I can place on the public notices, letters, reports of minutes, meetings and their chronology is that the plain design was preferred and Thomas Bradley was responsible for it.

Who was he and was he a native of Halifax? There is a fair amount to be discovered about him but it is a matter of argument as to whether the pieces we find refer to the same man. Beginning at his end, so to speak, the Halifax Reference Library has the following record of a gravestone in Square Church graveyard:

> *"Thomas Bradley, Civil Engineer and Jane his wife, the latter died 18 July 1814 (aged) 61 years and the former died 4 Feb 1833 (aged) 81 years. He was appointed Engineer to the Calder and Hebble Navigation Company in 1792 and discharged the duties of that Situation with great ability as well as the utmost integrity and zeal of the interest of his employers."*

Now if this is the Bradley of the Piece Hall then at the time of the publication of the 'Manufacturer's' letter in December 1774 he would have been just 22 years old. This is improbably, but not impossibly, young for a man to design a very large and costly building. As he became Chief Engineer to the Calder and Hebble Navigation Company, (the Canal Company referred to earlier in the manufacturers dispute over which site to build the Hall on), he must have been an able man. In his book, 'The Canals of Yorkshire and North East England, Volume One', Charles Hadfield wrote of him:

> *"Bradley, who built the new Fall Ing works (for the Calder and Hebble) was a very respected engineer. He had been taken on in December 1792 at £105 per annum. By 1803 he was earning £400 per annum and receiving donations from time to time and in 1819 the Company gave him £500 'as*

3. C.f. Leyland's account above. Leyland's article further stated: 'Mr. Bradley's plans and specifications had been, therefore, gladly accepted almost at the outset by the committee of trustees appointed for the purpose . . .' and 'The desired meeting was held on the 11th of February 1775, and it was then that Mr Bradley's design for the Hall was unanimously agreed upon'.

12

13

12 A later engraving of the garden front of Crownest.

13 'Square' Independent Chapel, 1770, drawn 'T. Bradley DELIN.', 1772. The Piece Hall was built just above it a few years later.

some remuneration for his past long and valuable services', added £100 per annum to his salary and promised him a pension of £200 per annum when he retired."[4]

Another reference occurs in Pigot's Directory of 1829 which lists a 'Thomas Bradley, Civil Engineer, of Union Street, Halifax', presumably a reference to his post with the Calder and Hebble Navigation Company.

Before joining the Calder and Hebble, Bradley's career is less certain. Richardson's 'The New Vitruvius Britannicus', published in 1802, contains drawings and the following description of an attractive, though modest English Palladian house designed by a Thomas Bradley in 1788, near Halifax. *10 11 12*

"Principal Storey of Crownest House near Halifax in Yorkshire. The seat of William Walker Esq., Thomas Bradley, Architect. Engraved London December 25th 1801 by George Richardson."

"This building is situated about three miles from the town of Halifax in Yorkshire at a little distance from the Turnpike road leading from thence to Wakefield and stands upon the site of an ancient family house which was taken down with all the out offices adjoining. This building is very much admired both for the beauty of the stone and the excellency of the workmanship.

The whole of the building including the wings is of stone of the finest quality and colour producing the most pleasing effect. The distribution of the apartments is allowed to be as convenient as most houses of the same size. The principal rooms are all finished in a style corresponding in every respect with the external appearance, taste and liberality of the worthy proprietor. The workmanship of this edifice in all its different branches is not to be surpassed, if equalled, by any in the country. The first stone of this building was laid in July 1788."

The owner of the house, William Walker, had been a signatory of the merchants' open letter that appeared in the Leeds Mercury on June 7th 1774 urging the quarrelling manufacturers to decide in favour of the Talbot Croft site[5].

Going backwards beyond 1788 the next reference to Thomas Bradley is in December 1776 when, in his marriage to Jane Appleyard, he gave joiner as his occupation. His wife's first name and the ages of both tally with the information on their gravestone, so here, there can be no doubt of the identity[6].
Then, in 1772, a 'T. Bradley' drew the 'Square' Independent Chapel which, we recall, was erected on *13*
Caygill's Talbot Croft, a few years after the building of the 'Square' of houses. The picture was published *49*
in 1789 in Jacob's 'History of Halifax' and shows an ability to draw and displays an interest in architecture. A 'Thomas Bradley' next appears in the Public Records Office in 1758 when he was apprenticed to his father who was described as 'a joiner of Halifax'. If this is the same Thomas Bradley of the gravestone, then in 1758, remembering that he died aged 81 in 1833, he would have been 6 years old.

Finally, the Parish Registry contains the record of his birth:

"Baptised June 1753 at Halifax Parish Church Thomas, Thomas Bradley, Halifax, Joiner"

Simple comparison of his date of birth and death shows a difference of 81 years which corresponds exactly to the age recorded on his gravestone. We remember that the 'Manufacturer's' letter of December 1774 referred to the designer of the plan most favoured by the manufacturers as being 'a native of this Town' and 'your own Townsman' and Thomas Bradley certainly seems to have been that. If we further accept that Thomas Bradley of Crownest, and Thomas Bradley of the Calder and Hebble, are one and the same then with his evident skill as an architect and engineer in later life we could, if we imagined, see him as the talented son of a joiner learning the rudiments of building and draughting to the point where he was able to produce a design for the Piece Hall which his fellow townsmen could

4. The Calder and Hebble employed good men. Their first engineer, John Smeaton joined them after designing the Eddystone Lighthouse – a structure famous for its use of concrete to form foundations under water.
5. Perhaps Bradley's commission for the house derived from the building of the Piece Hall? William Walker was also one of the proprietors of the Calder and Hebble Navigation Co. in which position he would have been Thomas Bradley's employer. 'Thomas Bradley master-builder' R. Spink Halifax Evening Courier, April 22nd 1978.
6. They had a son, William, who succeeded his father as an architect much as Thomas appears to have followed his father as a joiner. 'William Bradley and the building of Coley Church', R. Spink, Halifax Evening Courier, April 29th 1978.

describe as 'useful, elegant and plain'; despite the limitations of an architectural training in Halifax, and his young age of 22 years, such an interpretation is credible and is the one which, I think, most plausibly fits the facts.

But could the young, untrained Bradley really have had the architectural knowledge to go beyond the 'useful, elegant and plain' and create the classical Piece Hall with its detailed and eccentric language? His youth and inexperience make this questionable though it cannot be overlooked that Garside's account of the building of the Piece Hall does report him advising conformity with the principles of Roman classical architecture – though, at that time, few in the building trade would have advised any other style.

Then, of course, there is the reference to Hope as the architect at the foot of the song sheet. If, as we have seen, the Hope brothers were not involved in the first stage, and their role in the second has been described as that of general contractor and builder, how did they, or one of them, come by the title of architect? As masons we gather that their Estimate was part of a tender for Bradley's design but we know that the mason's contract, for the south side at least, went to others. Though this would not rule them out as masons for the remainder of the works, clearly, if they were, perhaps, one of only several subcontractors, it is hard to see how they would have been able to achieve such pre-eminence that the 'Hope' of the songsheet could be described as the architect. One other possibility remains. The Articles of Agreement referred to the appointment of an Architect and Surveyor to superintend the works. Could the Hopes, as builders and contractors, have been this architect and surveyor and, if so, was their detailed estimate the equivalent of a bill of quantities? If the Hopes were, indeed, appointed to one, or both, of these positions then it can be easily imagined how during the subsequent four years of construction Bradley's initial primacy could have been eclipsed and would help to account for the transformation of the Hall from the 'useful, elegant and plain' into the elaborate classical work of the finished building. It would also explain why 'Hope' became the metaphor with the specific meaning of 'architect' instead of, as Roberts expected, 'architects' (since the 'Articles of Agreement' refer to the position in the singular).

Who were the Hopes? There seems to be a confusion of two pairs of contemporaneous Hope brothers, both named Samuel and John. The first pair are listed in Colvin's 'Biographical Dictionary of British Architects', 1978; John Hope 1734-1808 and his brother, Samuel Hope 1737-1770. As Samuel Hope died c.1770 and the 'Estimate' of the Piece Hall was signed 'Samuel and John Hope' in 1775, this would appear to rule them out as the signatories. However, Colvin writes of them:

> *"They were the sons of John Hope, an architect and builder of Millington, near Altrincham in Cheshire. The father is said to have designed 'several Residences' in Cheshire and in particular to have been employed by the Earl of Stamford at Dunham Massey and Enville Hall (Staffs). His sons succeeded to his practice but moved to Liverpool in about 1763. In 1769 they competed jointly for the Royal Exchange in Dublin, but Samuel's death soon afterwards left John to carry on the practice alone for over 30 years. He died in 1808 in his 73rd year leaving his practice to be continued by his son-in-law William Byron. From 1770 onwards he kept a detailed diary of both his private and professional matters whose present whereabouts is unknown, though it was still in existence in 1869 (Builder, XXVI, 1869, 781, 803-4, 9090).*
>
> *In 1766 John Hope designed a vaulted room in the Liverpool Exchange in order to contain the Corporation Records, and in 1777, when it was proposed to build a new gaol, he was authorised to send for plans of Newgate Prison, London 'as lately rebuilt'. In 1773 he made an unexecuted design for the front of Enville Hall Staffs. for the 5th Earl of Stamford, and at about the same time one for Gwydyr Castle, North Wales for the 3rd Duke of Ancaster. He designed the Piece Hall at Halifax, Yorks. (D. Linstrum, 'West Yorkshire Architects and Architecture' forthcoming), the Bluecoat School at Warrington Lancs. in 1779-82, rebuilt High Legh Hall, Cheshire for Henry Cornwall Legh and altered Rode Hall, Cheshire for Randle Wilbraham c.1800. In 1802 he was employed at Ince Blundell, Lancs. by Henry Blundell, probably as executant architect of the latter's new Pantheon*

Gallery. In 1789 the tower of St. Nicholas Church, Liverpool, was repaired by Thomas Wainwright under his directions and in 1803 he was paid £2. 14s. 6d. for planning alterations to the same church.

In 1790 his designs for St. John's Church, Wakefield, were rejected in favour of those of Charles Watson but in 1794 he designed Holy Trinity Church, Wavertree near Liverpool with a prominent classical steeple in the Wren tradition."

In including the Piece Hall in the list of works attributed to these Hopes, Colvin is probably wrong. His source is Derek Linstrum's book, 'West Yorkshire Architects and Architecture'. Linstrum's information came from J. S. Roberts who, in turn, quoted details of John Hope's life from the first 1954 edition of Colvin's biographical sketch (which made no reference to Samuel Hope or the Piece Hall) to complete an apparent circle of misunderstanding between the three men.

However, the Hopes who are much more likely to have worked on the Piece Hall appear in a very helpful footnote to Colvin's biography of the above Liverpool Hopes. He writes:

"The Hopes of Liverpool must be distinguished from Samuel and J. Hope, statuary masons of Manchester, for whom see R. Gunnis, 'Dictionary of British Sculptors 1660-1851', 1968 p.208. Samuel Hope of Manchester was described as 'architect' in the Gentlemen's Magazine when he died at Altrincham in 1817 aged 76 (Gent's Mag. 1817, p.568). As the Liverpool Hopes were natives of Millington in the same parish, the two families were no doubt related."

Gunnis writes of them for the years 1780-1801:

"Their monuments and tablets, which are well designed and quite ambitious works with well carved details, include those to Anna Legh c.1780. at Rostherne, Cheshire; Mary Sayer, 1781 and John 14 15
Caygill, 1787, both in Halifax Parish Church; Hugh Hall, 1788 at Bourden, Cheshire; John Clegg, 1789 at Goostrey, Cheshire; Margaret Toosey, 1795 at Stockport, Cheshire; Thomas Drinkwater, 1797 at Salford, Lancs.; and James Brown, 1801 in the Parish Church of Ashton-under-Lyne. The later works are signed only by Samuel Hope."

I would add that John Caygill's monument of 1787 is signed only by Samuel Hope. This direct link with Halifax is even more interesting when we recall that John Caygill was the man who gave the land for the Piece Hall to be built on and that their only work east of the Pennines was in Halifax Parish Church[7]. Surely the link between these Hopes and Caygill is more than one of coincidence.

Though the Hopes' only work of clear authenticity has been till now of monuments and tablets, that Samuel Hope at least (but presumably John as well) aspired beyond statuary masonry is shown by his obituary in the Gentlemen's Magazine, dated May 1817, page 568.

"At Altrincham, aged 76, Mr. Samuel Hope, late of Manchester, Architect."

The rest of the obituary is an unhelpful testament to his worthy character with no details of his professional life.

However, documentary evidence of his and John's professional evolution is provided by a useful memoir written in the 19th century by a Mancunian called Owen[8]. The memoir contains the Manchester Directory for the years 1772-1804 faithfully copied out. The following years are taken from it:

1772	Hope, John, Surveyor and Builder, Alport Lane.
	Hope, Samuel, Snr., Builder and Bricklayer, Alport Lane.
	Hope, Samuel, Jnr., Surveyor and Builder, Alport Lane.
1773	Hope, John, Architect and marble cutter, Brazenose St.
	Hope, Samuel, Snr., Builder, 82 Deansgate.

7. Their link with the Halifax area began before 1775 when on April 20th 1773, as recorded in the Manchester Mercury, both Samuel and John married, John to a Leeds girl. John must have liked Yorkshire girls for a year after his wife's death, 1783, he married another Leeds woman.
8. Manchester Central Library. Owen MSS vol. 34 pp100-101.

14 The funerary monument to Mary Sayer, 1781, signed 'S. & J. Hope Fecit Manchester', Halifax Parish Church.

15 John Caygill's monument in Halifax Parish Church signed 'S. Hope Fecit Manches.', 1787. The urn is similar to the one over the Tuscan North Gate of the Piece Hall.

Hope, Samuel, Jnr., Architect and marble cutter, Cumberland St. 1774.
1774 (The same as the earlier entry for 1773.)
1775 (The same again except that Samuel Jnr. was also described as a stone cutter and builder. John was not mentioned.)
1776 (The same as 1775.)
1781 Hope, John, architect and marble cutter, Brazenose St.
Hope, Mr. Samuel Snr., 2 Deansgate.
Hope, Samuel Jnr., architect and marble cutter, Cumberland St.
1788 Samuel Hope, surveyor, marble and stone cutter, 12 Brazenose St.
1794 Hope, Samuel, architect and prop. of Garton Lime, 12 Brazenose St.
1800 (The same as 1794.)
1802 (The same as 1794.)
1804 Hope, Samuel at Queen's St., Deansgate House, 13 Ridgefield.

Clearly these Hopes, described as marble cutters, correspond with Gunnis's statuary masons; as surveyors and builders they would have had the knowledge of costs and materials to compile the detailed 'Estimate' of the Piece Hall; already described as architects in 1773, they fit the metaphor of the Piece Hall songsheet and since both were very definitely alive in 1781 to sign Mary Sayer's funerary monument they would have been quite able jointly to sign the 'Estimate' in 1775. It would seem from this that the Manchester Hopes have a far stronger connection with Halifax and the Piece Hall than the Liverpool Hopes whose only link is their name. However, though I think this interpretation is correct, it cannot be taken as categoric and some doubt must be allowed to remain[9].

But if we put aside this doubt for the moment, and accept the arguments for the respective roles of the Manchester Hopes and Thomas Bradley, it would be rewarding to set them in the context of the building industry in the 18th century. All three seem to have shared humble craftsman backgrounds but to have succeeded in their careers to the superior status of professional architect. John Summerson described the London building industry in his book 'Georgian London' and the picture it reveals of the relationship between builder and architect and the transformation from one to the other as the century progressed corresponds to Bradley and the Hopes very well. He writes:

> *"The building trade consisted, firstly, of craftsmen trained in a variety of different crafts – carpenters, joiners, masons, bricklayers, plasterers, glaziers, plumbers, carvers and paviors. These men were apprenticed for seven years, worked as journeymen, and then perhaps set up on their own. The system was still more or less medieval, except that trades were no longer closely organised even in towns. Although the City of London still had its Companies which were able to control the craftsmen within the City itself, the majority of men working in the expanding districts outside were not organised in any way.*
>
> *The London craftsman was, as a rule, a man of considerable skill and status – proud, conscientious, and expensive. He lived well and drank heartily. He was capable of writing a fairly good letter and could usually (if he were a mason, bricklayer, or carpenter) make a plain 'draught' of a small building.*
>
> *But his social importance did not end there. In the building trade, as in almost every other, there was, at the beginning of the eighteenth century, a strong capitalist element. The capitalist in the building trade was the 'master-builder'. Usually either a carpenter or a bricklayer by training, he would undertake the construction of entire houses and build for the speculative market. He was not necessarily (for reasons which we shall see in a moment) a great employer of labour but he was of the greatest importance because he took the initiative in building; as his point of view – the point of view*

9. For instance, the 'Manchester and Salford Directory' 1815-20, lists John Hope of 6, Swan St. Manchester under 'Architects' (Colvin). Which Hope can this be? Clearly not the statuary John Hope who did not live to sign Caygill's monument in 1787. Nor can he be the Liverpool John Hope since he died in 1808 and left his practice to his son-in-law William Byron. Perhaps he is the son of one of the Manchester Hopes carrying on after his father as Thomas Bradley's son did?

of the businessman rather the craftsman – became dominant, skill and originality became of secondary account. The constructional trades – bricklaying and carpentering – became businesses, and the trades requiring taste and good workmanship – joiners and carvers, for instance – became largely dependent on these.

If the master-builder was the central figure in the building trade, he was overshadowed socially, if not financially, by the SURVEYOR. The surveyor was what we should call a black-coated worker. As a type he was descended from the surveyors of Tudor times – products of the agrarian revolution; he was qualified not only to survey land but to supervise building work and measure it for estimating and pricing.

Lastly there was the ARCHITECT. But it cannot be too strongly emphasized that until half-way through the eighteenth century there was no such thing as an 'architectural profession' in the modern sense. The high-sounding title, 'architect', was adopted by anyone who could get away with it. Architects were recruited from tradesmen, from surveyors, and from the gentry. Good posts in the Royal service were open to them, though the word 'architect' was rarely attached to these offices, which were mostly surveyorships and clerkships of works, or offices nominally assigned to masons or carpenters.

Architecture was open to all. A Vanbrugh or an Archer might come to it as gentleman with a passion for building and under an obligation to find themselves a 'place' (Archer's 'place' incidentally was the wholly non-technical sinecure of 'groom-porter'). On the other hand, many of the most distinguished architects were trained as craftsmen. Flitcroft was a joiner by training, Ripley a carpenter, Kent a coach-painter. A writer of 1747, speaking of architects, says: 'I scarce know of any in ENGLAND who have had an Education regularly designed for the Profession. Bricklayers, carpenters, etc., all commence [i.e. set up] as Architects; especially in London, where there go but Few Rules to the building of a City-House.' One often finds a man described as Mr So-and-so, carpenter, becoming in a very short time So-and-so, Esq., architect. 'A pox on these builders – architects they call themselves', says one of Wycherley's characters, and it is, in fact, often impossible to tell whether the plan and proportions of a house were designed by an architect or a superior craftsman.

Speculative building and the architectural profession were the two goals of success for men entering the London building trade. The roles might be, and often were, combined. But the man who was temperamentally fitted for the more academic and literary parts of the business usually contrived to find himself a patron, with whose help he advanced along the road of pure professionalism as far as a country estate of his own, a carriage, a coat-of-arms, and a fortune of £10,000 or £20,000 . . .

The ability of the craftsman to better himself by becoming an architect or a quasi-architect provided a strong inducement to self-education, even to the more commercially-minded man, for he could not afford to be behind in questions of taste. Self-education meant getting a hold on the artistic needs of the centres of fashion. It meant the desertion of traditional craftsmanship and the adoption of certain academic formulas. Competition made this necessary; for with the growth of capitalism in the building world the individual either had to make a place for himself or remain a journeyman all his days at a wage of 12s. or 15s. a week under conditions which became rapidly less tolerable as time went on.

Thus we find the building industry transforming itself from a homogeneous body of independent craftsmen to a body comprising, at the top, the speculating master-builder, at the bottom the journeyman, and between the two, but on a pedestal of his own, raising him socially above either, the architect. The loss of status to the individual craftsman is obvious. He had to go into business as a speculator or get himself a patron and become an architect, or perish. To stand on his own feet he had to be something of an architect himself. This he was able to do through the medium of books." [10]

With what we know of the background of Bradley and the Hopes, Summerson's description becomes very interesting. We can now understand how Bradley's apprenticeship as a joiner may well

10. C.f. 'The beginnings of the architectural profession in Scotland'. Howard Colvin, Architectural History, Vol. 29: 1986. From this account the building industry in the 18th century Scotland was similar to Summerson's London and, I presume, the situation in rest of the country.

have trained him to be able to prepare a draught of a building, making it quite possible for him to produce the 'plain and simple design' of the Piece Hall. And though in his subsequent career he did not find a great patron or place, at least he had one wealthy client, the wool merchant William Walker, and found a final, if prestigiously modest, post with the Calder and Hebble Navigation Company.

Whether the Hopes, in later life, were similarly successful is obscure but clearly they too proceeded down the path of professional advancement. As to their involvement with the Hall, from their earlier work as both builders and surveyors, Summerson's description of these occupations dovetails with the interpretation of their role that they arrived in Halifax after the acceptance of Bradley's design, prepared and submitted their Estimate for the publicly invited tender and were then appointed to superintend its construction as the architect and surveyor – Bradley being at 22, too young and inexperienced to hold either job[11].

Whether they then had a hand in the design of any part of the Hall is hard to judge. From their funerary monuments they obviously could both design (or copy) details as well as carve them and perhaps they were influential in the specific selection of the classical detailing. But if their Estimate was made wholly from Bradley's 'plain design,' which it seems to have been, then their function can only have been the translation of Bradley's design into information from which it could be built and then to superintend the work on site. Summerson tells us that builders often simply changed their title to architect without altering the actual nature of their work. In this light we do not have to see 'Hope' as the designer of the entire project (as a modern architect would usually be), or even a part of it, merely because the song sheet called one of them 'Architect'.

And here we will have to leave the engaging matter of the authorship of the building; Bradley apportioned with the credit of its general design and the Hopes responsible for its construction and maybe its details as well. It is possible, I think, to dwell too much on this question. Perhaps more interesting than the things which may divide their responsibilities are the similarities of their beginnings and development, particularly their common moves from craftsmen to architects. For in this they parallel Summerson's outline of the 18th century building industry in London. The essential instrument that accomplished this career transformation he ascribes to books and this is a very important idea for us because, as we shall see in due course, the relationship of architectural books to Bradley, the Hopes and the Piece Hall appears to be similarly crucial.

In the design of any building at any period there are many circumstances which affect or determine its eventual form, only one of which (though very important) is the individual ability and predilection of the mind of the 'architect'. If books were a major influence another must have been the cloth halls of rival towns which preceded the Piece Hall. The clear characteristics of the design of these form a long tradition and it is difficult to believe that Bradley, at least, would not have been well aware of them. The extent and meaning of any direct effect they may have had on the Hall is discussed in the chapter which follows.

11. After sight of a preliminary draft of this book, Mr. Colvin has kindly confirmed to me that High Legh Hall was built, not by the Liverpool Hopes as he had recorded in his biography of them, but by a Samuel Hope, bricklayer, and John Davies of Millington, and the work was measured by one John Hope. He concludes that the Hopes of High Legh must be the Manchester ones (I assume because the Owen MSS. describes Samuel Snr. as a bricklyer, Samuel Jnr. as a builder and John as a surveyor). If this is indeed so, then the confirmation of the nature and division of responsibilities between them fits well with my view that one was the superintending architect/builder of the Piece Hall and the other was the superintending surveyor. One final point, since Gunnis' Dictionary credits the statuary Manchester Hopes with Anna Legh's funerary monument at Rostherne, Cheshire, was she connected with High Legh Hall, Cheshire, and did the Hopes commission for her monument derive from the building of that house as Caygill's memorial may have from the Piece Hall? Millington, Rostherne and High Legh are within three miles of each other.

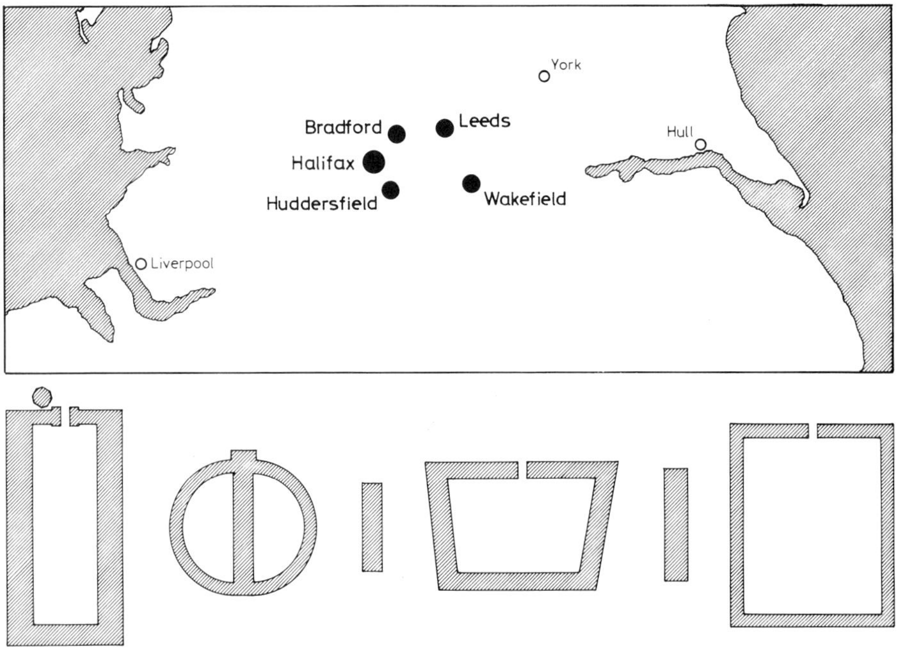

16 The neighbouring Cloth Halls in the West Riding of Yorkshire. From left to right, the Leeds Mixed Cloth Hall, 1758; Huddersfield Cloth Hall, 1766; Bradford Piece Hall, 1773; the Leeds Third White Cloth Hall, 1775; Wakefield Cloth Hall, 1778 and Halifax Piece Hall, 1779.

17 The entrance to Huddersfield Cloth Hall from Cloth Hall Street, 1930. The columned bell cupola and clock base resemble those of the Leeds Third White Cloth Hall **36**.

CHAPTER FOUR

The Cloth Halls of the Neighbouring Towns

If Bradley, or the Hopes, were newcomers to the design of cloth halls, at least they would have had to guide them a succession of halls built in the surrounding towns in the preceding two decades. These *16* formed one of the most important architectural influences that combined to create the Piece Hall for they contained the general organisation and some specific architectural features of the Hall at Halifax. All shared common reasons for their existence; sometimes they were built to escape the problems of weather and theft in the streets; sometimes where trade had grown the old hall became inadequate or they arose through the competition of a rival town's new hall. As each sought to attract as much trade to their town as possible, so successive halls became costlier, larger and more architecturally ambitious. This was not, however, a straightforward evolution since wealthy towns could build generously whilst small villages had to be modest.

The towns and cities of Huddersfield, Leeds, Bradford and Wakefield were the chief trading rivals of Halifax but of the many market halls built, only Halifax survives; fortunately sufficient accounts and descriptions remain to enable satisfactory reconstructions. The cloth halls of other local towns and villages, like Colne, Heptonstall and Gomersall, have disappeared and only references to them are made in their local libraries. They seem to have been of the same type as Bradford and Wakefield, however.

Huddersfield

Huddersfield had a similar history of cloth halls to Halifax but it is the last in particular which is important. It opened in 1766 and was built probably in response to the competition of the Second White Cloth Hall in Leeds in use since 1755. In quality of architecture Huddersfield was second only to Halifax but quite unique in its shape. In plan it was initially a single storey ellipse bisected by a long hall *18* with the main entrance in the east. Apart from the entrance, the building presented blank walls to the outside so affording protection from theft and fire. They were made of brick and articulated with an abstract buttressing pattern of strip pilaster and projecting stringcourse at the level of the floor and roof.

The interior was organised into 'streets' and private rooms. The clothiers had previously displayed their cloths on trestles in the town's thoroughfares and this arrangement had been transferred and formalised in their Hall. It was not uncommon for these 'streets' to retain their names in the transfer. A corridor 'street' of trestles ran around the periphery; the private rooms faced into the interior court. The central axial hall had an open layout of tables with roof support given by a line of monolithic stone Tuscan *20*
columns running down the middle. The interior court walls were articulated by arcading formed from a *19*
slight projection of the brickwork, enclosing round-headed windows. The main entrance had on its axis *17*
a modest Georgian house topped by the traditional cupola containing the bell rung to open and close the market. This was added in 1780 with the second storey. In 1848 further cross-axial rooms completed the division of the courts into quadrants. The Hall was demolished in the 1930's though the cupola, at least, was saved and now stands in Ravensknowle Park in Huddersfield; the remainder of the building *21* was used as rubble to build a road.

Ignoring their different shapes, Halifax and Huddersfield have much in common: both have exterior blank walls forming secure courts internally; both have individual 'shops' for each clothier organised along corridors; both have some form of arcading articulating their exteriors; both, though in different measure, have monolithic Tuscan columns and each is a formal design dressed with classical architecture. As an example of planning however, Huddersfield is rather inept. Its peripheral corridor must have been a mean and gloomy place and the two semi-elliptical courts created by the central hall formed no part of the building's circulation and could not have been used by anyone. Their sole purpose

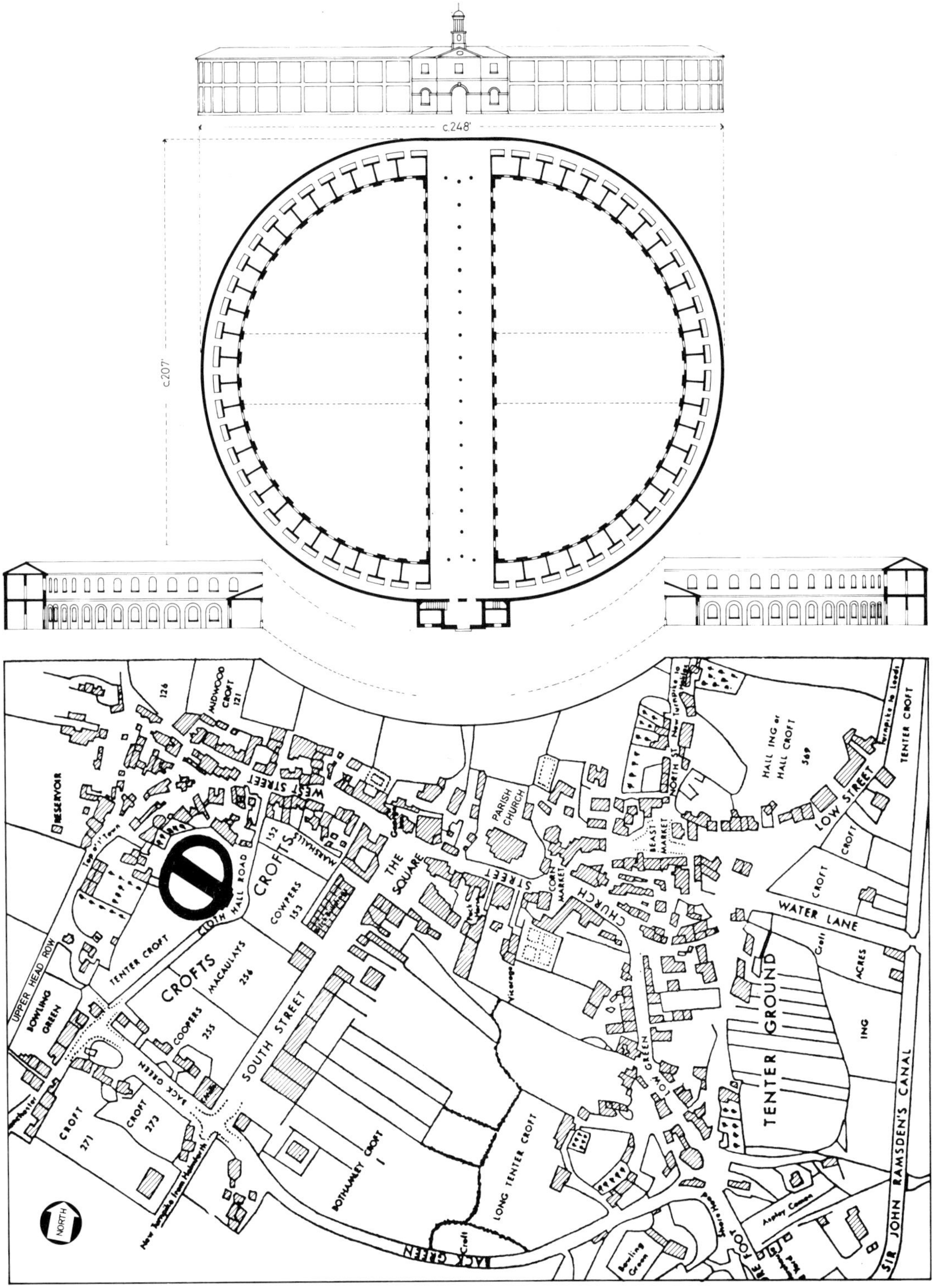

18 Huddersfield Cloth Hall, 1766, and Huddersfield in 1778. The Hall is shown after the addition of the second storey and front entrance in 1780. A further cross-axis of accommodation was added in 1848.

19

20

21

19 The central hall and interior court of Huddersfield Cloth Hall.

20 The interior of the main hall, Huddersfield, with the line of supporting Tuscan columns.

21 The columned bell cupola and clock base of Huddersfield Cloth Hall re-erected in Ravensknowle Park, Huddersfield.

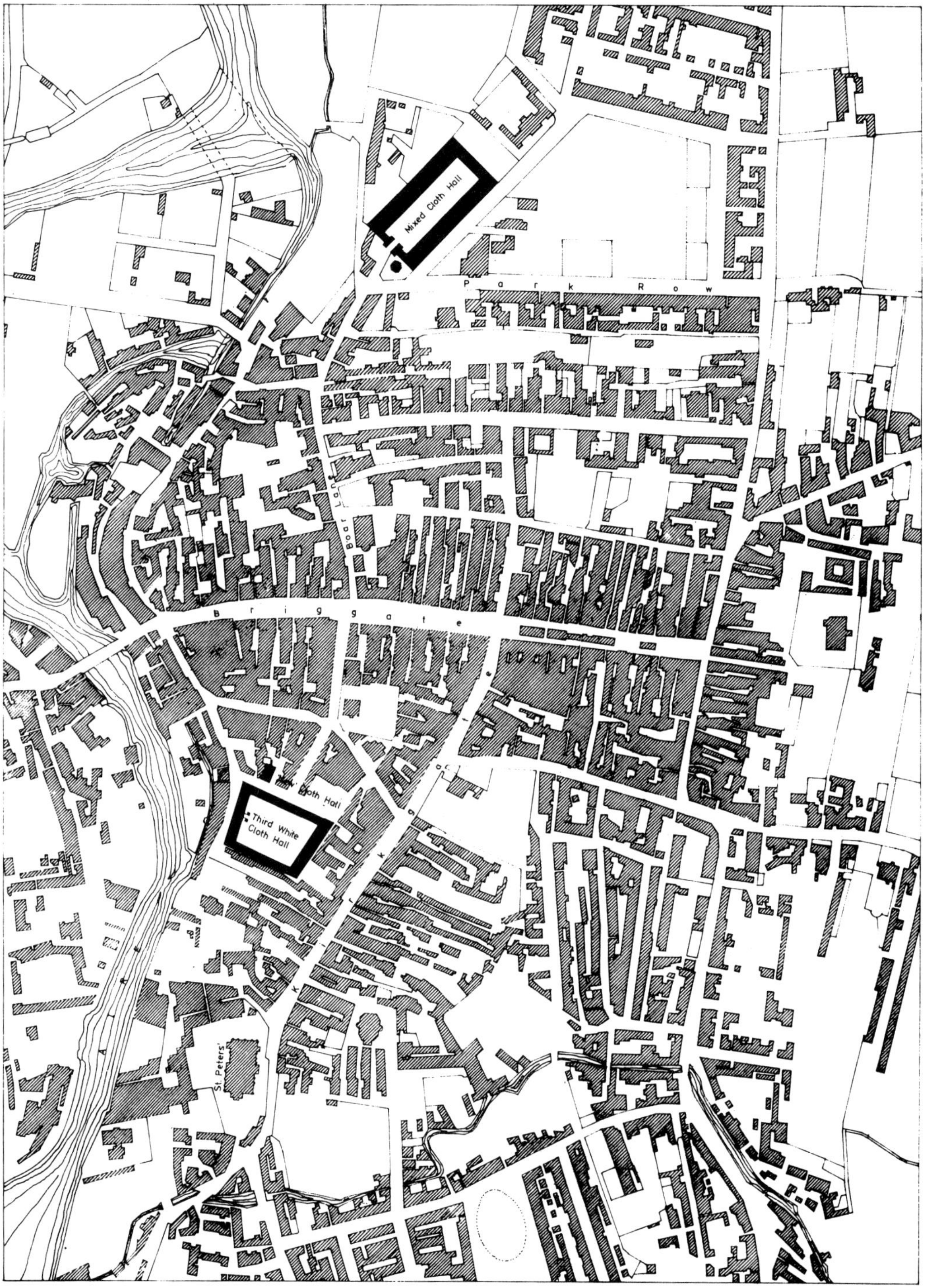

22 Leeds in 1815; the Mixed or Coloured Cloth Hall, 1756-58, and the Third White Cloth Hall, 1774-75. The First White, or New, Cloth Hall lies beside the Third White Cloth Hall.

was to light the rooms[1]. As for the elliptical plan, perhaps there was a strong preference for a unique and distinctive shape. It may derive from the contemporary popularity of the elliptical 'circus' as an architectural form. Rectangular halls were the norm, however, and those of Leeds, that follow, are important examples.

Leeds

Leeds replied to the competition of the cloth hall built in Wakefield in 1710 with its first cloth hall in
1711. It was a small two-storeyed building formed with arches and pillars arranged around a quadrangular
court; on market days, each floor was filled with stalls to display the pieces of cloth. Naturally, it had a
painted and gilded cupola and appears to have been an early, smaller version of Halifax. It is shown on 22
the Leeds map near the Third White Cloth Hall.

In 1755 it was succeeded by the Second White Cloth Hall built on a different site in the city. There
are no descriptions of its appearance. In 1758 it was followed by the 'Leeds Coloured' or 'Mixed' Cloth 23
Hall. Derek Linstrum in his book, 'West Yorkshire Architects and Architecture' writes of it:

> *"The largest building in Leeds at the time, it was designed by John Moxon and described as exceeding*
> *'any building of its kind in Europe'; in form it consisted of a large rectangular courtyard surrounded on* 25
> *three sides by single storey brick buildings and measuring one hundred and twenty yards and a half by*
> *sixty-six. There was an entrance in the middle of the fourth side and at the opposite end of the*
> *courtyard the five bay, pedimented central section was surmounted by a bell cupola. All the facades*
> *were plain, consisting only of regularly spaced large windows with segmental heads, although a gable*
> *or pediment broke the monotony in each of the long sides. The finest architectural feature of the group*
> *was built probably 25 years later than the Hall itself. It stood to the right of the pedimented entrance,*
> *as a detached octagon covered by a shallow dome and an arcaded cupola that was curiously* 24
> *Byzantine in form; this building, entered through a projecting porch, was the Exchange built for the*
> *convenience of the merchants and for transacting business respecting the cloth hall by the trustees. The*
> *domed interior was neatly decorated in a plain neoclassical taste, and over the fireplace hung a*
> *portrait of Edward III who was popularly believed to have introduced the woollen manufacture into*
> *England in the fourteenth century.*
>
> *The three wings of the hall were divided into 'six long streets or aisles' each containing two rows of*
> *stands two feet wide, where the clothiers stood to display their cloths in rough state to the merchants* 26
> *and finishers. The hall was built in such a position as entirely prevents 'the rays of ye sun or a blaze of*
> *light entering ye apartments in ye Winter or Summer Season till after ye time appointed for ye cloths*
> *being exposed to sale'. They could not show the cloth in a true light if the light was suffered to shine*
> *upon it."*

Here the organisation of a hall around a rectangular courtyard (though only on one storey) with stalls forming 'streets' in the interior reproduces the arrangement of business prior to the building of market halls. It is hard to say if the building originally looked both inwards to the courtyard, and outwards to the street but certainly windows were present after the addition of the second storey in 1810[2].

In 1774 the Third White Cloth Hall was built in response to the threatened competition of a new cloth hall in the nearby village of Gomersall. This came about through the initiative of the merchants rather than of the manufacturers. Larger than the Second White Cloth Hall, but smaller than the Mixed Cloth Hall, it was built on an irregular piece of land known as the Tenter Ground in the Calls. In the Leeds tradition it was arranged around a courtyard but, in following the site perimeter, it formed a trapezium in plan. Linstrum writes of it:

1. C.f. the Manufacturer's letter describing the Halifax circular hall, page 10.
2. It is likely there were no windows to the street as it is otherwise difficult to see how direct sun could have been excluded.

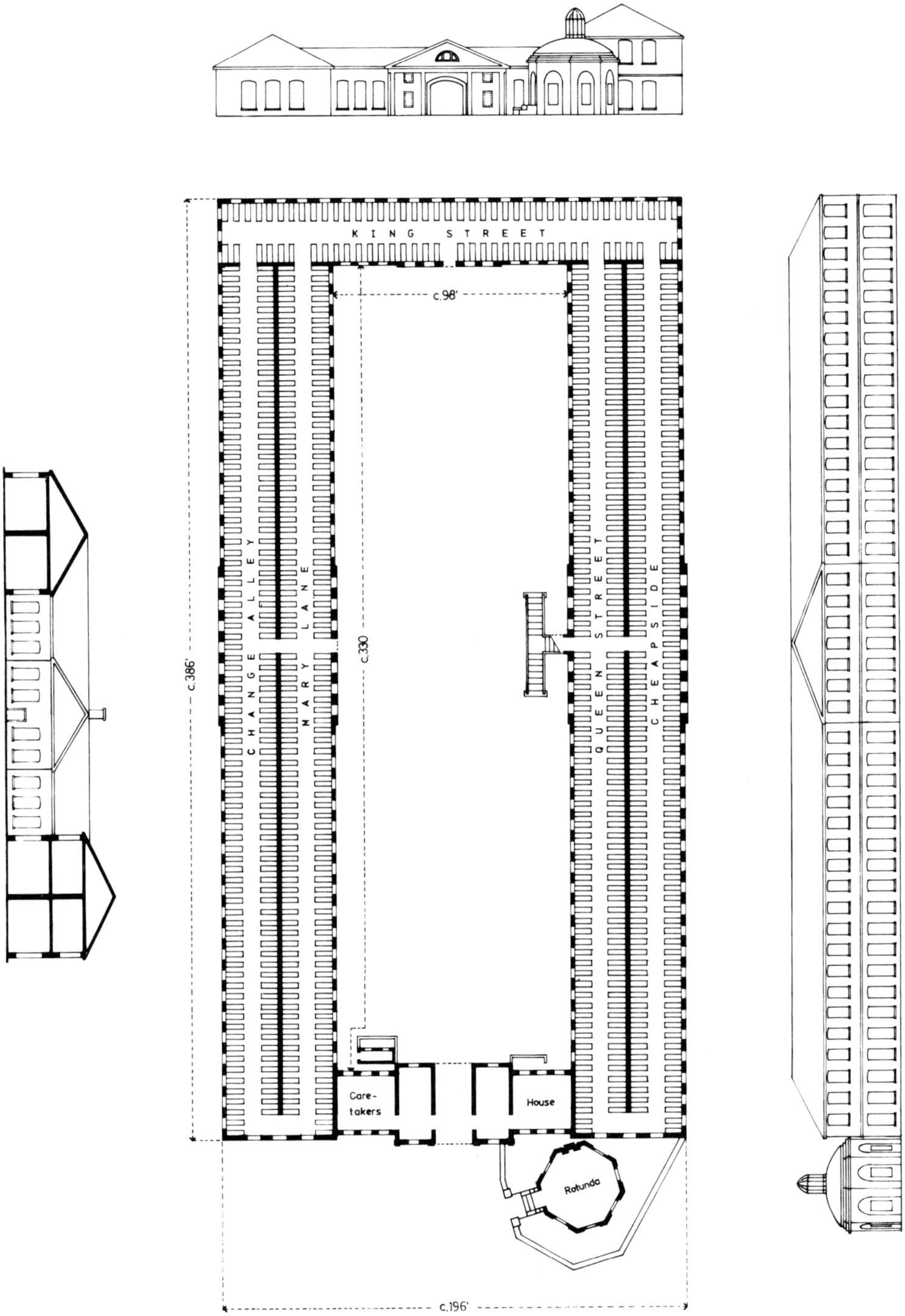

23 The Leeds Mixed or Coloured Cloth Hall, 1756-58, reconstructed in its final form; the Rotunda was added about 1783 and the upper storey, over 'Queen Street' and 'Cheapside', in 1810. To protect the cloths from direct sunlight there were originally far fewer windows.

24 The Leeds Mixed or Coloured Cloth Hall; the meeting room Rotunda and the upper storey of the Hall are later additions.

24

25

25 The Leeds Mixed or Coloured Cloth Hall yard.

26 The interior of the Leeds Mixed or Coloured Cloth Hall on market day. The street name of the old open air market, 'Cheapside', has been retained.

26

27 The facade of the Leeds Third White Cloth Hall, 1775, all that remains today. The blank arcading is similar to the Piece Hall.

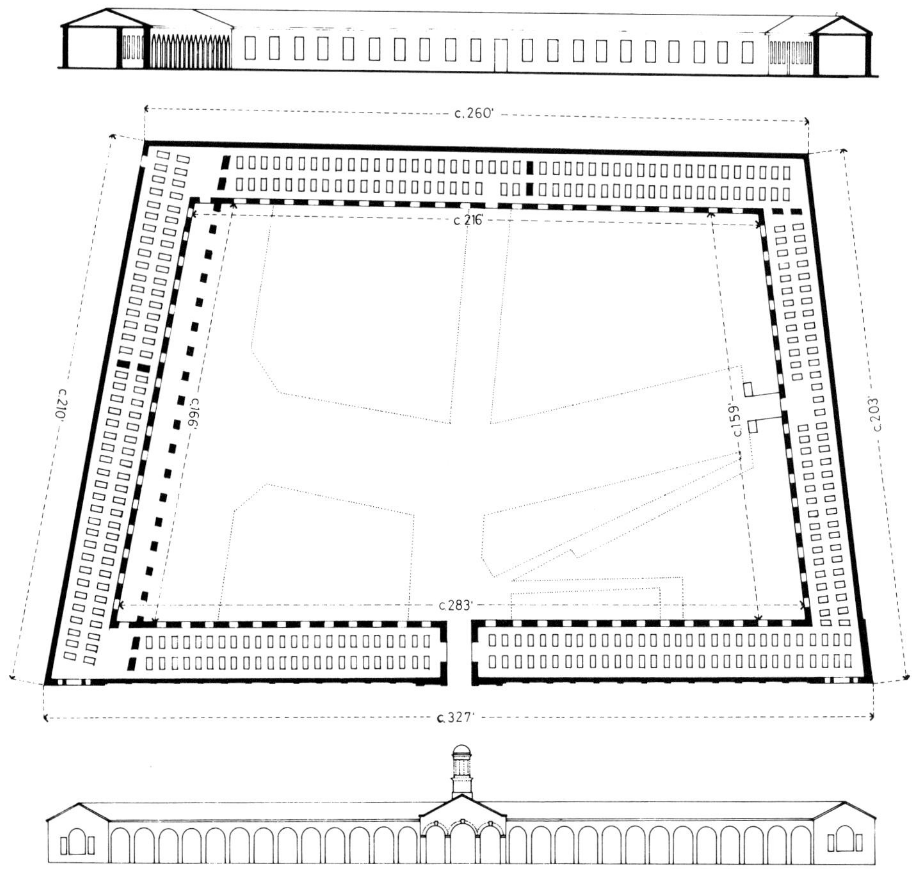

28 The Leeds Third White Cloth Hall, 1774-75. The building formed a trapezium in order to maximise its use of the given plot of land.

"... it was divided into five streets and contained 1,213 stalls. The main frontage still exists – a 27
plain brick facade with a central pedimented section crowned by a cupola containing a bell (both removed from the earlier White Cloth Hall) which rang to signal the opening and closing of the market. The facade which faced onto the Calls had a pedimented section of three bays at each side and terminating pavilions with Venetian windows. Possibly the designer was William Johnson who was
employed at Temple Newsam by Lord Irwin."[3] 28

It was fear of competition from the Third White Cloth Hall that moved the Halifax manufacturers to build their Hall and perhaps the connection extended to the architecture as well. For Halifax and Huddersfield share with the Leeds Cloth Halls the fundamental arrangement of an inward looking courtyard that presented windowless facades to the exterior. In some ways the relationship even encompassed particular elements, for instance the blank arcaded entrance facade of Halifax and the Third White Cloth Hall (though there are obvious differences of detail). Nor should the use of pillars and arches in the courtyard of the First White Cloth Hall be overlooked as a possible, and at that time still existing, model for Halifax.

The major differences are, most obviously, the organisation of internal streets and trestles contrasting with, at Halifax, the provision of private individual rooms or 'shops'. Particularly important is the fundamentally different attitude to design. Leeds built pragmatically with only a few decoratively applied features whereas Halifax is a building of coherent architectural order.

Though the Cloth Halls of Bradford and Wakefield are of no help as a source for this latter quality, they do provide the other part of the basic strategy of Halifax in their evolution and use of the individual 'room' for each manufacturer.

Bradford

The origin of the 'shop' arrangement, where each clothier had his own room within the cloth hall, can be seen in the trading practices prior to the erection of the Piece Hall in Bradford. The manufacturers brought their cloth to the town and exhibited it in a large room at the White Lion Inn, Kirkgate, which was divided into closets. Those who lived in the town had their own piece rooms in or near their houses. Only a minority displayed their cloth in the streets.

The old Bradford Piece Hall (pulled down long ago) is essentially that room at the White Lion, 29
built as a long rectangle and on two storeys. The Hall was opened in 1773 and cost £1,500 provided by Gentlemen, Merchants, Wool-staplers, Manufacturers and others. James Hartley, a local headmaster, wrote in his 'Old History of Bradford' in 1776 that it was:

"... a very elegant, and commodious Hall, about 50 yards in length and eleven broad, the lower room of which is divided equally into two, by a brick wall running from end to end of the said building. Against this wall, in these apartments, are fixt about 100 closets in a very commodious manner with shew board to every such closet to shew the goods upon, these closets are the property of such Manufacturers as at first subscribed, with power to transfer; in these closets are reposited goods from one market day to another. The upper room is also closeted, but upon a different plan, these are occupied by such as did not subscribe, paying a certain rent yearly for the use of them."

Though small, it still had a little cupola on the roof for the market bell and steps to the first floor on the outside, ornamenting the entrance.

Wakefield

Wakefield's first cloth hall was opened in 1712 and began the chain reaction of competition that culminated in the explosion of cloth halls in the 1770's. The available description of it is sketchy; it had

3. The 'Minutes of the Merchants Meetings for the New White Cloth Hall 1774-5' in the Dartmouth Estate Papers, Leeds City Library Archive Department, refer to a Mr Hawkswell and a Mr Lawrence being asked to prepare plans.

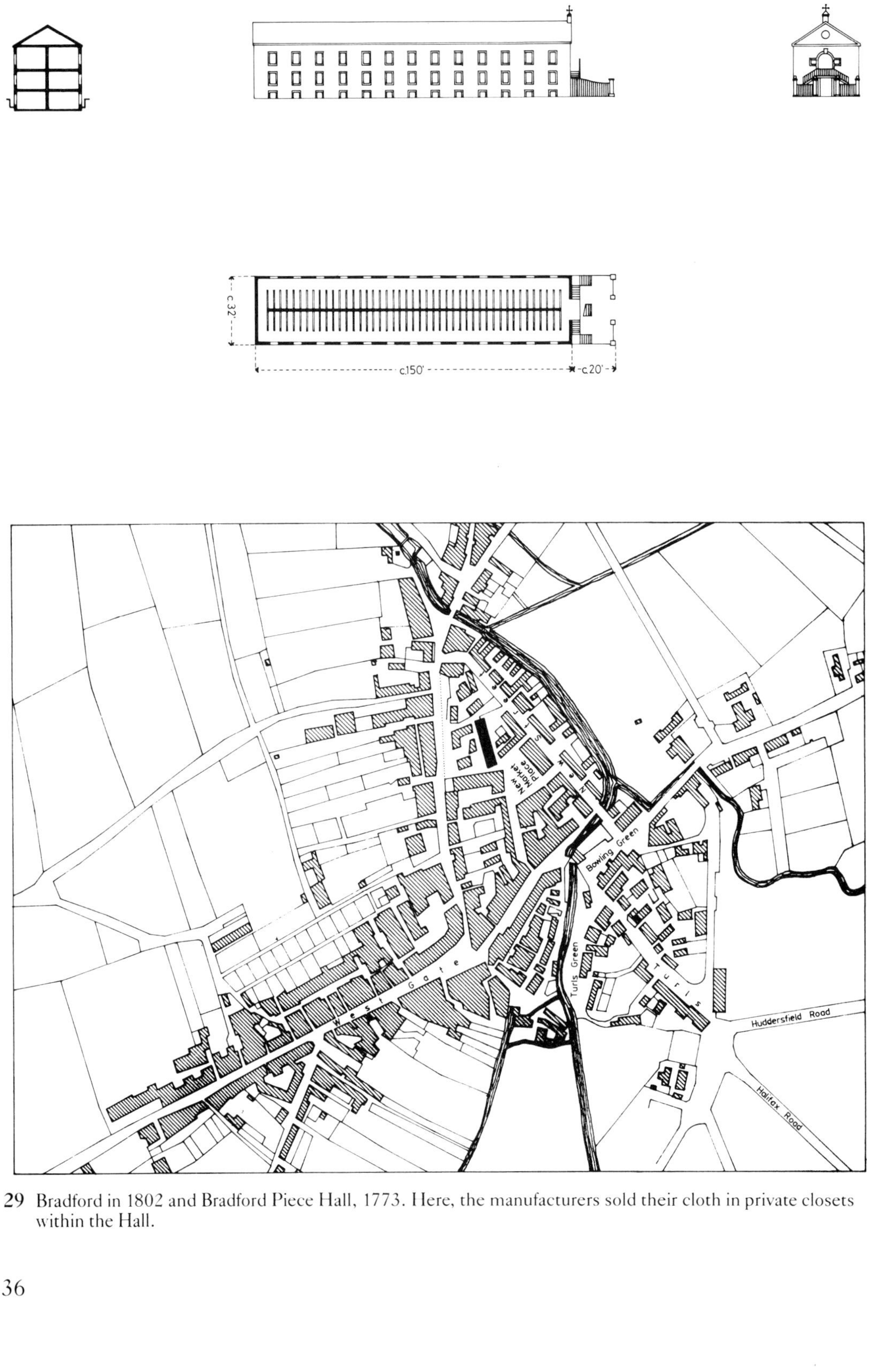

29 Bradford in 1802 and Bradford Piece Hall, 1773. Here, the manufacturers sold their cloth in private closets within the Hall.

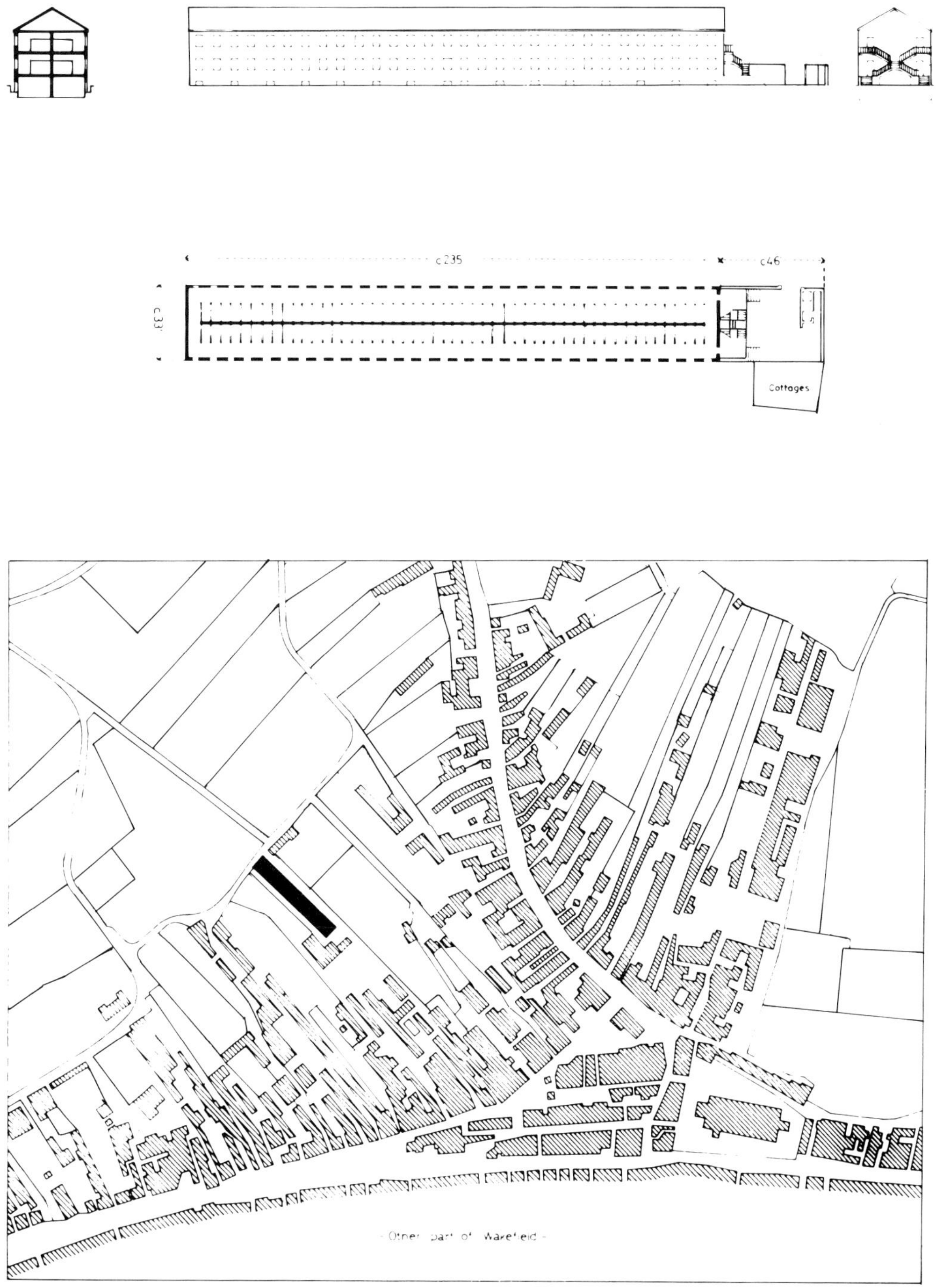

30 Wakefield in 1794 and Wakefield Tammy (Cloth) Hall, 1778. It is virtually identical to the Bradford Piece Hall.

two floors and may have been similar to the hall at Bradford. By 1731 it had been turned over to other uses.

30 There was a break of 40 years before another hall was built. There were about 140 subscribers to the new hall, each giving £8.8.0. to the 'Tammy Hall' (so called from the type of cloth sold) and in addition £1,000 from local merchants. In all the hall cost £2,176. Each member had his own stand or stall, arranged as at Bradford.

The Hall was opened on 10th July, 1778 – 6 months before Halifax. A description of 1876, prior to its extensive alteration, was made by a local historian, John Hewitt.

> *"The exterior was about 80 yards long and 11 yards wide. There was a double row of 30 windows (on each side). There were 16 cellar windows (on each side). There would be the same number of windows on the opposite side fronting into King Street. There was cellaring under the most part of the building but the principal portions were the two upper rooms with suitable offices within and these had been used for the selling in of the Tammys. They were about 9 feet only from floor to ceiling. The whole were approached by some flights of stone steps at the southern gable end the entrance to which was a small enclosed yard in which stood two brick cottages then inhabited. The steps were guarded with iron railings . . . The turret had seven pillars to it but there was no bell . . . the interior was ten yards in width . . ."*

Another description in the Universal British Directory c.1790 said of it:

> *"The stuffs are exposed to sale in an elegant hall erected about 15 years ago by subscription. It is two storeys high, extending in length about seventy yards, in breadth about ten. Through the middle in each storey is a row of repositories, in all about two hundred facing each way, properly labelled, so that the stand of any manufacturer may be easily found."*

Though Wakefield contained twice as many stalls (200) as Bradford and differed in small details, it had much the same organisation and appearance. Doubtless both Bradford and Wakefield were so utilitarian in articulation and form because there were fewer manufacturers and less was available for a rich and impressive display.

From this survey of the neighbouring cloth halls it can be surmised that Halifax's achievement was,
51 like Huddersfield, to fuse the 'shop' arrangement of Bradford and Wakefield with the large courtyard type
36 of Leeds. This combination united the advantages of general privacy and security from the outside
world given by the internal court with the seclusion and confidentiality between clothier and merchant
provided by the individual room. And Halifax, by learning from the example of Huddersfield, and not
putting the circulation on the periphery, with the rooms placed direct on the court, but instead, setting
37 the corridors on the court side and the rooms behind, allowed satisfactory light to the rooms whilst
affording full enjoyment and use of the great courtyard. No doubt we should credit Thomas Bradley's
'useful, elegant and plain' design with this economic but subtle and profound re-arrangement of the
essential elements of cloth hall tradition.

31 The Tuscan North Gate and flanking blank arcading.

32 The great courtyard: basement arcade, rusticated gallery amd Tuscan colonnade; behind are the individual rooms of the manufacturers.

33 The West Gate was formed in 1782 to ease congestion at the end of the weekly market. The bellcote was added in 1785.

34 The South Gate; originally small, it was enlarged in 1871 to allow vehicles to enter. The cast-iron gates date from this alteration. Through the arch can be seen the small entrance of the North Gate into the courtyard.

35 The South and West Gates from the courtyard. Their column spacings are marginally wider than the standard spacing.

36 The Piece Hall courtyard from the west with the blank arcading of the north elevation and the North Tuscan Gate. Behind the spire of Square Church lies Beacon Hill. Other than the entrances, the Hall has no openings or windows to the outside.

37 The Rusticated Gallery with the doors and windows of the individual manufacturers' shops on the left.

38 The Piece Hall from the east with the 'Square' Independent Chapel and the spire of the old Square Church in the foreground.

39 The three abutting Tuscan columns forming the courtyard corner.

CHAPTER FIVE

Architecture

Medieval Ancestors and Classical Prototypes, The Site and Courtyard Proportions, Pattern Books, Architectural Language, Theory and Lessons

Medieval Ancestors and Classical Prototypes

If the Piece Hall had done no more than combine the two main types of cloth hall of its rival towns, it would have remained a utilitarian structure much like them. In going beyond the purely practical it created a formal classical statement of remarkable architectural quality. The manufacturers had sought an 'ornament to the town'[1] and when completed could claim that it did indeed rival 'Palaces of Old'.

But which palaces? The prosperous European and British cloth trade had built many halls from the earliest middle ages but none resembled the Piece Hall[2]. The largest and one of the earliest was built at Ypres in the 13th century. It contained other functions besides the cloth market: the Town Hall, law *40*
courts, a prison and a chapel. Though large, c.435 feet long and two storeys high, it bears no resemblance to Halifax. There were others similar at Louvain, 1317 (200 feet long), and Courtrai (272 feet).

The general market at Saumur was an early example of an arrangement of shops connected by an arcade around a central space; this type has much in common with a monastic cloister. Filarete proposed *41*
something similar in his Italian Renaissance 'Treatise' in the 1460's. The Fondaco dei Tedeschi in *42*
Venice, rebuilt in 1505, in the Veneto-Byzantine style was another cloister arranged around a courtyard but formed from four levels of arched galleries. It was a general purpose building combining the functions of warehouse, wholesale market and living accommodation. Though there are general similarities between this cloister type of court and Halifax, Leeds and Huddersfield, there is no evidence to suppose that any direct link exists; after all an arrangement of shops around an open space is a common idea.

If there is no direct precedent for the Piece Hall in its medieval and Renaissance ancestors, where do we then look? We recall Maurice Garside's report of Thomas Bradley advising the Piece Hall Committee in the following manner[3]:

> *"Mr. Thomas Bradley, . . . , advised that the edifice should not only be of colossal proportions, so as to be well adapted for the primary use to which it was to be devoted, but also that it should conform in design with the principles of Roman classical archictecture as adapted to more modern circumstances by the greatest artists of the Italian Renaissance. Fortunately, Bradley seems to have been entirely uninfluenced by the decadent examples of the late Italian style, and took as his guide the work of Bramante and his followers."*

Garside (and Leyland[4]) suggested a resemblance with a Renaissance palace courtyard and cited

1. F. A. Leyland's 'Eighteenth Century Halifax: the Manufacturers Hall'. The Halifax Courier April 9th 1887.
2. This section is taken from Pevsner's 'A History of Building Types' – Chapter 15.
3. Maurice Garside 'Transactions of the Halifax Antiquarian Society' – 1921.
4. C.f. Leyland with Garside; "His advice was . . . that the edifice should not only be of colossal proportions, and be well adapted for the primary use to which it was to be devoted, but should also be designed in conformity with the principles of Roman classical architecture, as adapted to the more modern circumstances by the great artists of the Italian Renaissance prime. It is much to the credit of this able gentleman that, uninfluenced by the decadent examples of the late Italian style, whereof so many were before him in this country, he was able to take the art as exemplified in the works of Bramante and his followers, Christoforo, Roechi, Ventura, Vitoni, Rafaella and Baldassare Peruzzi of Sienna, and to fashion thereon a great public edifice that should be well-suited to eighteenth century needs".

40

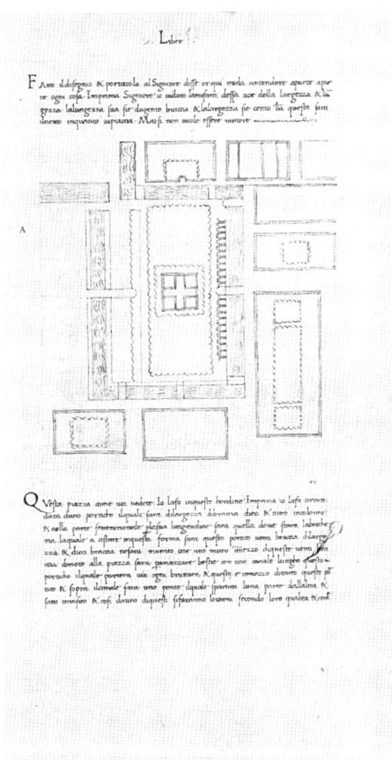

41

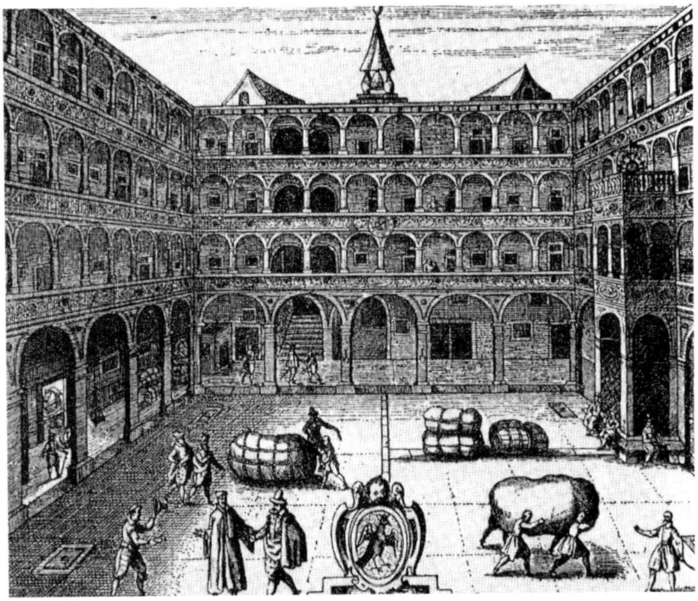

42

40 Ypres Cloth Hall, c.1260-1380.

41 Filarete, design for a market, early 1460's.

42 The Fondaco dei Tedeschi in Venice, c.1505.

43 The courtyard of Bramante's Cancelleria Palace, Rome, c.1486-1500.

44 The Forum of Proculus, or Caesareum, Cyrene, North Africa, late 1st century B.C.

43

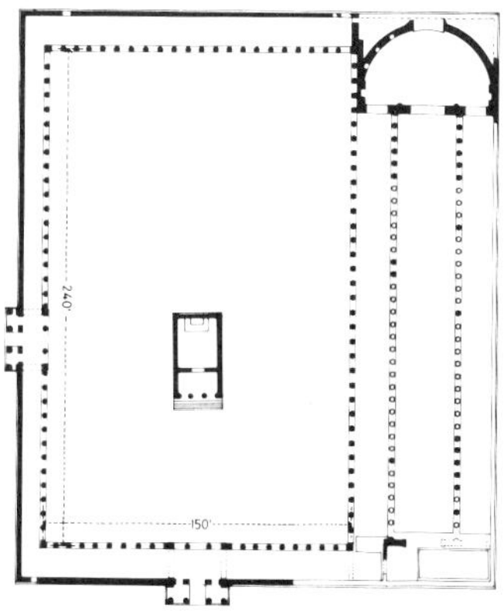

44

43 Bramante's Cancelleria Palace but the proportions and scale are so unlike those of the Piece Hall that
other than a topological similarity of columns and arcades there is little connection. The Cancelleria
courtyard is a small, tall square; the Piece Hall courtyard is a large, comparatively low rectangle and
comprises many more bays.

If Bradley did indeed advise conformity with the principles of Roman Classical Architecture as
adapted by the great architects of the Italian Renaissance, then a more credible comparison (and one
44 suggested by J. S. Roberts and others) would be with a Roman Forum; a large, relatively low, quadrangle,
created from superimposed columns of enclosing galleries, inward looking, a place of meeting and
business. Where might Bradley have found examples of such buildings and acquired his apparent confident familiarity with Italian Classical and Renaissance architecture? 18th century Britain abounded in books of architectural theory, illustrating the works of the authors and those of the ancient Romans. Who knows whether the young Bradley or the pragmatic Hopes knew of these books? The ideas and engravings they contained conjured the image of classical Italy before the imagination of both patron and architect; in any building enterprise it was inescapable. As we saw earlier, books were the means whereby craftsmen such as Bradley and the Hopes were able to effect the transition to architect. They were the essential practical texts of their trade and no doubt the relatively experienced Hopes would have ensured their access to them. But where would Bradley have been able to obtain theoretical works? T. W. Hanson's 'History of Old Halifax' records the unexpected presence in Halifax of the following:

> *"One of the most famous bookshops in the kingdom was that of 'Edwards of Halifax'. William Edwards, the father, 'was for many years very eminent in his profession, and of no common estimation for the energies of his mind; and his skill in collecting rare books, not less than his exquisite taste in rich and expensive bindings, will long be recollected'[5]. He died in 1808. James Edwards, his most famous son, who opened a London bookshop in 1784, was the first London bookseller to display valuable books in splendid bindings."*

We do not know whether they dealt in the books we are concerned with but the prestige of their trade is comparable with the elaborate and costly productions of contemporary architectural literature.

Of the many published in England before 1774 only two contain buildings similar to the Piece
Hall[6]. Leoni's 1726 English edition of Alberti's 'De Re Aedificatoria' includes a short chapter on the
45 46 forums of the Greeks and Romans and reconstructs a free-standing Roman forum very similar to the
Piece Hall. Palladio's chapter 'Of the Piazze of the Romans' (Third Book, Chap. XVIII) in the 'Four
Books of Architecture' is closely based on Alberti's earlier work and from his own archaeological
47 48 investigations also reconstructs a 'Piazza' which bears close comparison with Alberti's (though it is
contained within a group of buildings).

Both books are fundamentals of European architectural history. The Florentine, Leon Battista Alberti (1404-72) is arguably the greatest of all theorists. His Renaissance work sought to secure the modern foundation of architecture and raise the standing of the architect from that of manual craftsman through an appeal to the authority of the Ancients and to the principles of the Universe. As we shall see, an equivalent, though far less elevated, transformation was to take place in 18th century England but there the appeal was not to be to the Ancients but instead to the prestige conferred on the Italian Renaissance by men such as Alberti.

His thesis, divided into ten books, ranged from arcane theory to an elucidation of the most practical aspects of building; it is a staggering edifice of thought. The first edition was published in 1485 in Latin and without illustrations. It was not until 1550 that the meticulous, verbal descriptions of buildings in his text were transposed into woodcuts by one Cosimo Bartoli. In England the book did not appear until 1726. The translated and illustrated edition, by the naturalised Englishman Giacomo Leoni, not only changed the title to 'The Ten Books of Architecture', but also redrew Bartoli's woodcuts, considerably embellished in the Baroque spirit. My reproductions are from this edition but it must be remembered that in style, they are as far from Alberti as they are in time (300 years). This almost

5. 'Edwards of Halifax', T. W. Hanson, Halifax Antiquarian Society Transactions, 1912.
6. See bibliography.

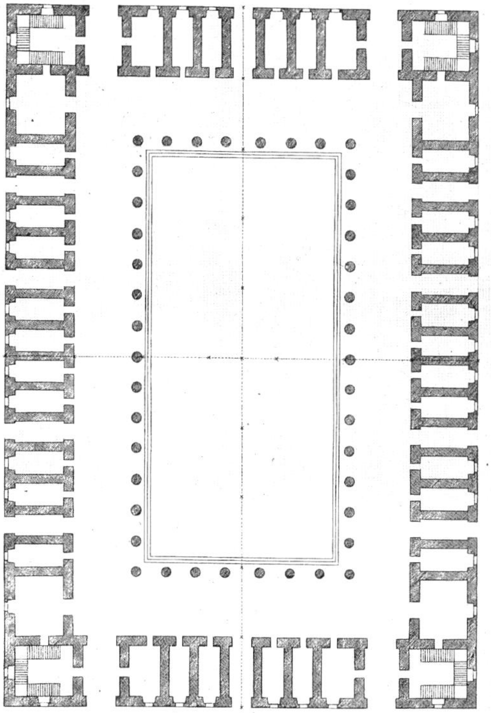

45

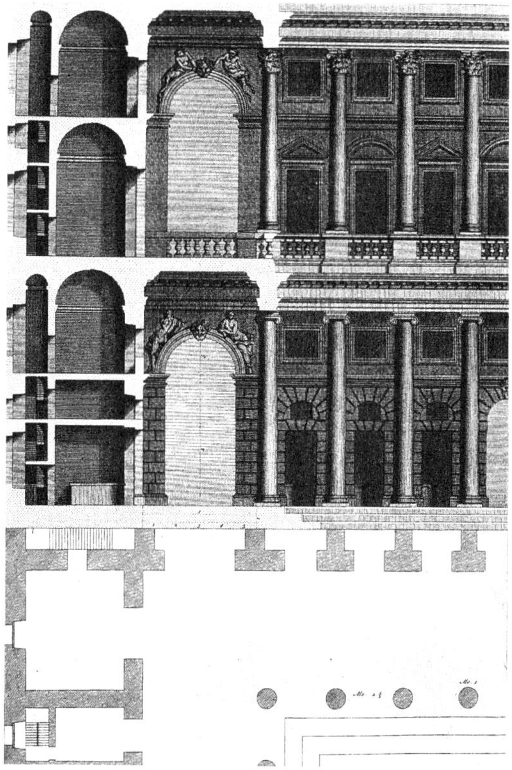

46

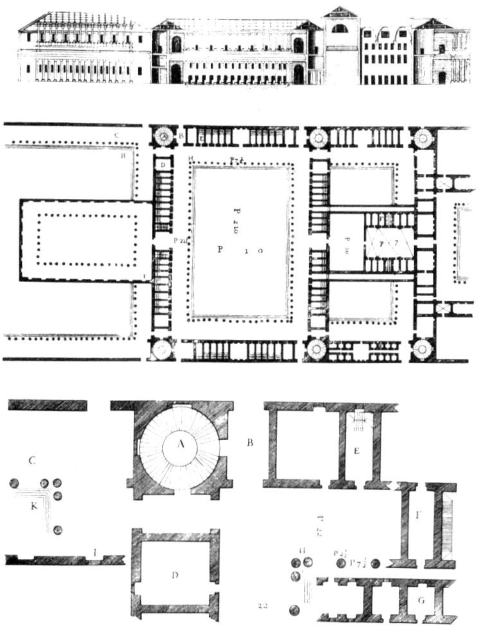

47

48

45 Alberti's 'Roman Piazza' from Leoni's translation of his 'De Re Aedificatoria', 1726. The courtyard is a double square.

47 Palladio's reconstruction 'Of the Piazza of the Romans'. The central courtyard has a proportion of 1:3.

46 Part elevation of Alberti's 'Roman Piazza'.

48 Part elevation of Palladio's 'Roman Piazza'.

automatic process of returning to earlier classical tradition and then unself-consciously reinterpreting it for contemporary purposes is a major characteristic of classicism and one which finds more than an echo in the Piece Hall.

Alberti was born a gentleman, Palladio (1508-80), like the Hopes, began as a stonemason. He is one of the most famous and influential architects of history both through the inspiration of his many built works and his theoretical treatise. His 'I Quattro Libri dell' Architettura' placed a greater emphasis on the practice of architecture than Alberti's but the thought behind it is very much a development from him. The book contained illustrations of all his built and unbuilt projects and of his sometimes fanciful archaeological reconstructions of ancient Roman buildings. From its first publication in Venice in 1570, its importance was recognised and subsequent editions and translations spread throughout Europe. Inigo Jones introduced the first copy to England after his visit to Italy in 1614 but it was not until 1715 – 135 years after Palladio's death – that the first English edition appeared. Once again Leoni was responsible but, as he was to do with Alberti's treatise, the illustrations were redrawn in his own manner with additions and even misinterpretations. Though an edition, scrupulously faithful to the original, was published by Isaac Ware in 1738 (from which my reproductions are taken), human nature being what it is, Leoni's corrupted version proved to be more successful.

The 'Four Books' (the translated title) had extensive influence in Britain from 1715 onwards. Its popularity was greatly helped by its propagation in the revolution of taste created by Lord Burlington and William Kent, in their reaction away from the opulent, dramatic baroque of Wren, Vanbrugh and Hawksmoor, to a more restrained – and in their opinion – more decorous classicism. If not entirely a Bible of the new movement the 'Four Books' could be considered a kind of architectural New Testament. For this reason it would be a far more probable source for the Piece Hall than the 'Ten Books of Architecture'.

In comparison of general design both 'Piazze' have many obvious similarities to the Piece Hall; a multi-storeyed courtyard, windowless to the outside with repeated modular shops opening off the interior colonnades, stairs at each corner and, in the example of Alberti, free-standing. The obvious anomalies are the three storeys of the Piece Hall, the sloping site and the different classical orders used.
39 Though in the arrangement of three abutting columns at each corner, the Hall is the same as Palladio, in other details – door arrangements, ornamentataion and so on – it mostly differs from both.

45 47 50 This is also true of proportions. Where Alberti has a courtyard of ratio 1:2 and Palladio 2:3, the
46 48 Piece Hall has 4:5. Where Alberti and Palladio's columns are tall and close together (2½ and 2¼ diameters) the Piece Hall's are short and well spaced (5¼ and 6 diameters). Palladio's walkways were as wide as the height of the columns, the Piece Hall's, like Alberti's, are much narrower but all three have column spacings which correspond to the room spacings. Alberti and Palladio have many entrances, the Piece Hall, as originally built, only one.

If the Piece Hall is based on Alberti or Palladio, then it has been much modified since the similarities are those of general principle not detail. But, as we have seen in the reproduction of their books, modification, whether deliberate or not, appears to have been an inherent quality of their dissemination. If this could happen in the more academic sphere of publishing, how much greater was the scope for variation in the world of building. In this it is intriguing to remember the relationship of John Wood to classical Rome and his misunderstanding of the forms and functions of the circus and amphitheatre to recreate them as the Royal Crescent and the Circus at Bath. If this 18th century archaeological misinterpretation gave rise to Bath, perhaps the re-worked inspiration of ancient precedent extended to Halifax as well[7].

The Site and Proportions

49 More obviously the circumstances of the site must have had a considerable influence on the design of the Hall. We recall that John Caygill gave the land for the Hall to be built on and that this was

7. John Summerson's 'Heavenly Mansions' 1963; John Wood and the English Town-Planning Tradition'. Wood mistook a Roman circus (a long rectangle with semi-circular ends used for chariot races) for a Roman amphitheatre (in fact an ellipse in shape) turned the 'amiphitheatre' inside out (his model seems to have been the Colosseum), made it circular and used it for housing instead of gladiatorial bloodsports.

49 The plan of Halifax about 1779 reconstructed from two earlier plans, **86** and **87**, using a 1922 Ordnance Survey Map as an accurate base. The enlarged plan of Caygill's Square shows the Piece Hall before the creation of the West Gate into Vicar Field in 1782.

doubtless to complete the open fourth side of his 'Square' of houses . The quality and formality of the 'Square' must have suggested a comparable response from the Hall since an undistinguished building would have appeared inadequate. Hence the northern side became the entrance facade not only through being the closest to the town centre, but also because it fronted the 'Square'. With handsome Tuscan gateway and blank arcading, it was the sole articulated facade, the other bare elevations faced only open countryside.

Significantly the Hall also derived its alignment from the 'Square' but its exact placing in relation to it is less straightforward. The given plot of land is described[8] as 110 yards from north to south and 99 and 19 yards from east to west. The meaning of the 19 yards is obscure; perhaps one end of the site was 19 yards longer than the other. North to south the Hall was the full site length – 110 yards – but east to west it was only 90 yards – at least 9 yards short of the boundary. This raises two questions; firstly, did the spare site lie to one side of the Hall, or the other, or both? That is, what governed the exact location opposite the 'Square'? Secondly, in not occupying all of the site[9], what determined the size and proportion of the plan? Were abstract rules applied or did practical constraints dominate?

The north facade was set back from the end of the mansions on the lower, eastern side by some 15 yards. This was, of course, determined by the line of the site boundary. The only specific relationship of the Hall with the 'Square' to be seen is the axis just passing to one side of the mansions opposite. This probably means no more than that was where the road was. The only general correspondence apparent is the complete closing off of Caygill's 'Square' on its south side. However, it is a lopsided relationship since the western half of the Hall's north elevation lies entirely beyond the 'Square' itself.

Architectural sense could have been made if Caygill had intended to reproduce the arrangement of mansions on the upper western side of the Square, so placing the Piece Hall on the axial centre. This would have been very difficult to achieve as it would have involved the demolition of the Assembly Rooms in the north west corner. In any event it never happened. Various buildings were built along the road to the entrance gate soon after its opening (including the porter's lodge) and eventually reached the north elevation so cutting it, visually, in half. Certainly, as the Square was left by the building of the Hall, it had little unifying geometry or order. Rather it appears to have been not much more than a tidy grouping of old and new building.

The factors determining the specific size, proportion and shape of the plan are far from clear. Compared to the amount of accommodation required, the area of the site was large enough to allow a certain latitude in the form of the Hall. As we have seen, a circular hall was proposed but even more obviously a square could have been chosen. Why then a rectangle? Since the surrounding buildings did not suggest or compel a rectangular form the reasons must lie somewhere between architectural
23 28 29 preference and physical limitations. Doubtless the rectangular tradition of Leeds, Bradford and
30 Wakefield had some effect. Any bias they may have imparted would have been reinforced by the steep fall of the site and sandstone bedrock immediately beneath the surface. We remember that the Hall extended the full length of the site north to south, that is perpendicular to the slope and so relatively unaffected by it. However, in the opposite direction, the wider the building became, the more basement was required. In fact, the Hall cut in slightly to the ground on the upper west side and the basement arcade on the lower eastern side had to be built up. To have become wider still, would have incurred more excavations and foundations. As it was, the accommodation requirement was satisfied just before the width of the building matched its length.

But it is clear from measurement of the courtyard that the final size has not been left to the accidents of the site and the simple requirements of the brief. We might expect a rigorous classical building, as the Piece Hall appears to be, to be governed by a proportional system that not only generated all the overall proportions but those of the constituent elements and details as well. Certainly
50 there are some regular proportions in the Hall and the clearest of these belongs to the great court. The

8. F. A. Leyland 'Eighteenth Century Halifax: the Manufacturers' Hall'. The Halifax Courier April 9th 1887.
9. As the Leeds Third White Cloth Hall did; it followed the site boundaries and so formed an irregular shape.

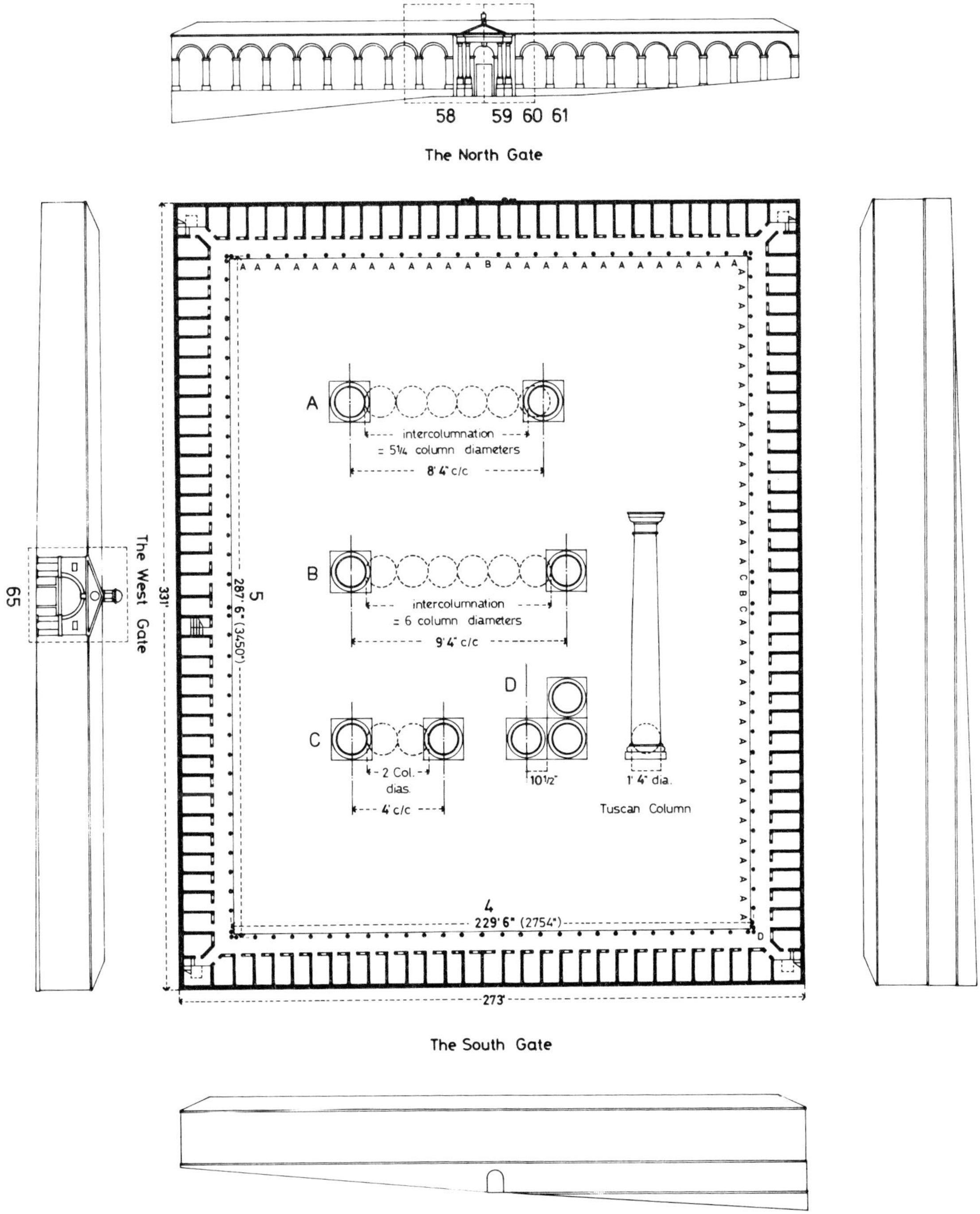

50 The Tuscan Gallery plan (upper level) and external elevations. The Hall is shown as it was in 1782 after the West Gate was created but without the enlarged South Gate (formed in 1871).

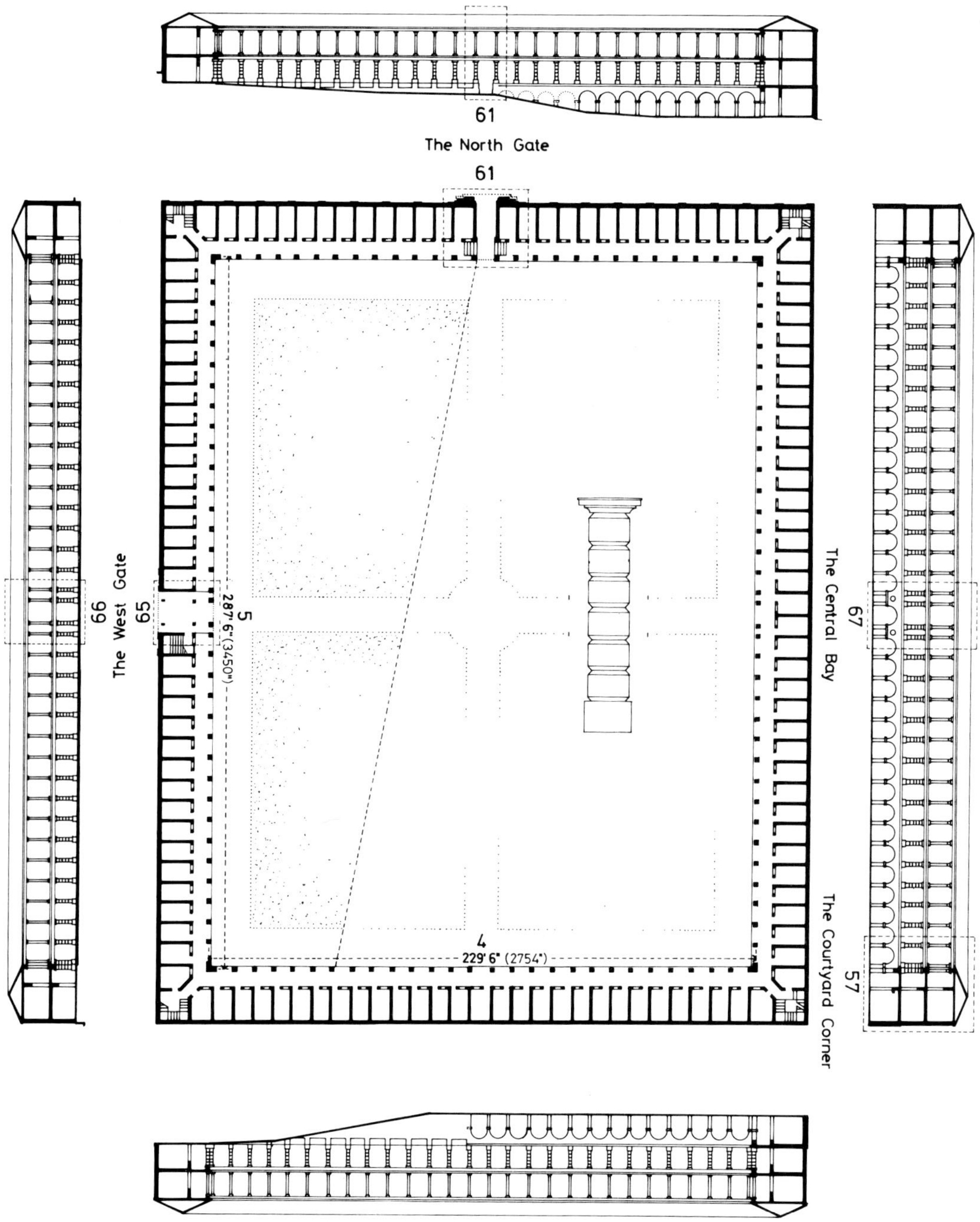

51 The Rusticated Gallery plan (ground level) and internal courtyard elevations and sections. The Hall is shown as it was in 1782 after the West Gate was created but without the enlarged South Gate (formed in 1871).

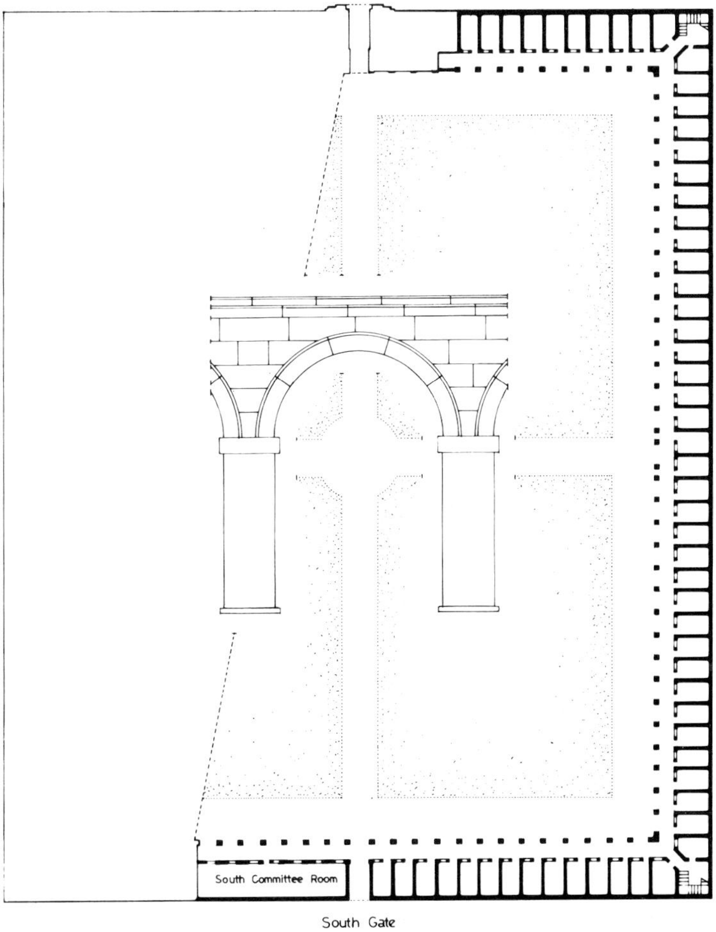

52 The Tuscan Arcade plan (basement level). The Hall is shown as it was built in 1779 with the room arrangement of door and window as the floors above (the arched openings we see today are not original) and without the enlarged South Gate (formed in 1871).

width from the centre of each corner column/pier equals 229′ 6″ (2754″) and that of the length, 287′ 6″ (3450″). Width and length are in the ratio of 4:5[10].

The source and meaning of this ratio is a matter of conjecture. Palladio, as we have seen specifically recommended a proportion of 2:3 for his reconstruction of a Roman Piazze and Alberti 1:2. For rooms Palladio advised the alternative shapes of a circle, a square, a square and its diagonal, a square and a third, a square and a half, a square and two thirds and a double square. At 4:5 the Piece Hall is a square and a quarter and so belongs to this family of numerical relationships. Though he did not single out this proportion, Palladio did in fact use it for rooms and the proportions of whole buildings.

Alberti and Palladio's proportions derive from the ancient Pythagoreo-Platonic discovery of the relationship between mathematics and music[11]. When they had made this discovery the Ancients thought they had found the secret of the Universe, and the Italian Renaissance agreed with them. The Renaissance architect, in proportioning his buildings in accordance with this number system, felt that his building was in harmony with the divine order. Traditionally represented in the shape of a Lambda,

1
2 3
4 9
8 27

The harmony of the world is expressed in the seven numbers, 1,2,3,4,8,9,27, which embrace the secret rhythm in macrocosm and microcosm alike. For the ratios between these numbers were believed to contain not only all the musical consonances, but also the inaudible music of the heavens and structure of the immortal human soul.

The system reached full development in the musical theory of the Italian Renaissance during the
5.3 15th and 16th centuries and from a reconstruction of a contemporary diagram of the 'harmonic division of the octave into its parts' the ratio of 4:5 is revealed, in musical terminology, as a major third. The complete system is too extensive to present in detail but for our purposes, brief examples of the three essential proportional mechanisms will suffice to convey its sophistication. The first, the arithmetic mean is, however, very simple, for example;

6 : 9 : 12

here the middle term is always the 'arithmetic mean' between the first and last terms. The second mechanism, the geometric mean, is more complex;

4 : 6 : 9

in this sequence a constant ratio of 2:3 between the terms is introduced. That is, 4 is to 6, as 6 is to 9. The third mechanism, the harmonic mean is the most subtle;

6 : 8 : 12

the notion of ratios between the three terms is taken a step further, that is, the difference between the second and first term is 2, and 2 is one third of 6. Similarly the difference between the third and second term is 4, and 4 is one third of 12.

All three proportional means are coherently interrelated along the harmonic scale but they could be interpreted by different architects to produce different proportional results. However, they would always be recognisably whole number ratios of the above kind. If the proportion of 4:5 is evidence of the conscious presence of the system in the Piece Hall we would expect to find similar ratios elsewhere in the building.

10. 2754″ requires an extra 6″ to correspond precisely to this ratio; however over such a distance, so small an inconsistency has not been considered significant.
11. Much of this section is based on Rudolph Wittkower's 'Architectural Principles in the Age of Humanism, Part Four: The Problem of Harmonic Proportion in Architecture', 1949.

53

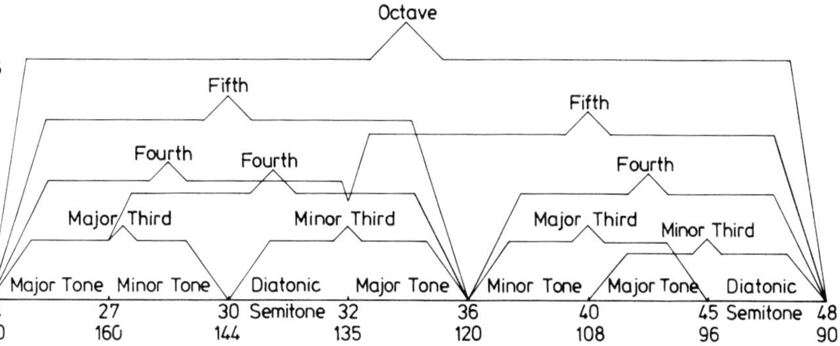

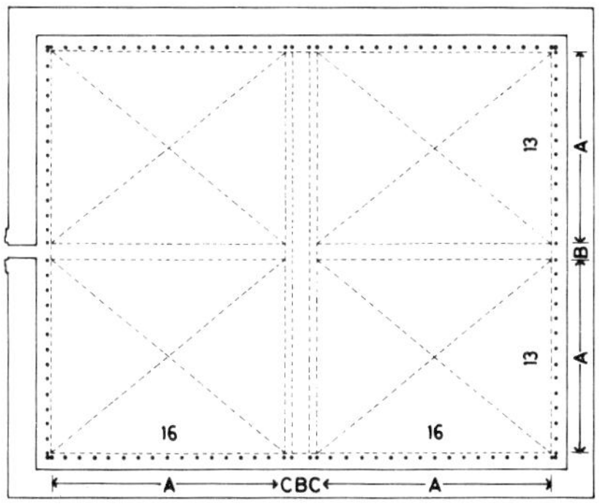

54

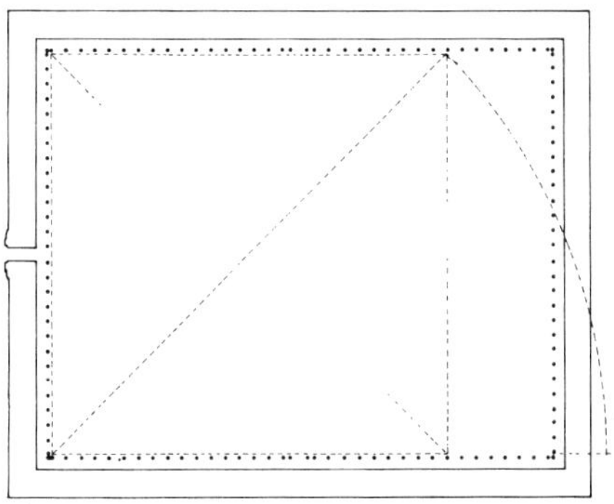

55

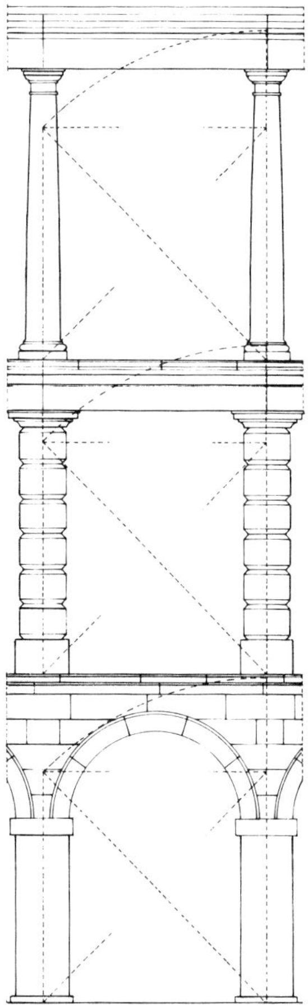

56

53 Zarlino's 'harmonic division of the octave into its parts', mid-16th century.
54 Proportional analysis of the courtyard column spacings.
55 The courtyard is not the Golden Section proportion formed by a square and its diagonal.
56 Apart from, possibly, the basement, the Golden Section is not found in the courtyard elevation.

The proportional system was explained in part in Plato's 'Timaeus' and in considerable obscurity by the Augustan Roman architect, Vitruvius, in his work 'De architectura'. Vitruvius' treatise was the only complete architectural text to survive from antiquity and consequently was held in great esteem by the Renaissance, particularly Alberti and Palladio; their respective 'Books of Architecture' were modelled directly on this. A full and clearer exposition of the Vitruvian thesis was published in the Italian Renaissance theorist Francesco Giorgi's 'Harmonia Mundi' but it cannot be conceived that Bradley or the Hopes would have known this work or, indeed, those of Plato and Vitruvius. The one work they are most likely to have had, Palladio's 'Four Books' is of no help either for though Palladio and his circle were fully familiar with the system, in the 'Four Books' he only makes cryptic references to the particular proportions he uses. To anyone unfamiliar with the full system these cryptic notes are indecipherable.

In fact the only book that would have been available which propounded a clear description of the system and its correct application, was Leoni's edition of 'De Re Aedificatoria'. In Book IX, Chapter V establishes the authority of numbers and Chapter VI explains the arithmetic, geometric and harmonic proportions; Chapter VII goes on to enunciate the relationship of column diameters to their heights. As
45 46 we have already seen, Leoni's edition contains the one design most like the Piece Hall. Whether Bradley, or the Hopes, availed themselves of this book with its 'Piazza' and proportional system, I do not know. If they did, it would be quite extraordinary, but however remarkable, we cannot ignore that both are there in the book.

As the Renaissance progressed, application of the system became increasingly sophisticated. The most astonishing example, where the system was minutely applied to every detail, occurred not in an actual building, but in a reconstruction of Solomon's biblical temple, by the scholar Villalpando. In more usual operation, however, the system was applied only to some of the shapes of a design – for example to the overall building block, to the window and door openings and to the columns and entablature of the order. In 18th century Britain, even erudite theorists had only an imperfect grasp of it and, in contrast to the exemplars of Renaissance Italy, proportional relationships seem to have been applied in theoretical works, pattern books and general practice to the elements of the building rather than the composition as a whole. With the growth of scientific empiricism the system lost its divine authority though for a time its prestige was maintained by the deep respect felt for the great architects of Classical and Renaissance Italy. In turn this authority passed away in the desire to break free of its constrictions. By the 1770's the whole structure of classical aesthetics had been methodically dismantled and the system was neither common academic knowledge nor common building practice even among eminent architects. Proportion became a matter of individual sensibility and has remained so to this day.

Examination of other elements in the Piece Hall for corroborating evidence of proportional meaning gives, at best, an ambiguous picture and the diameter of the Tuscan column is a good instance
50 of this. The predominant intercolumnation in the Tuscan colonnade is 5¼ diameters. Such a fractional
48 46 sum is not unusual; in Palladio's Corinthian and Ionic Piazza the module is 2¼, in Alberti 2½. For the Tuscan order itself Palladio used 4, and the English architect, William Chambers, 7 – choice seems to have been a matter of personal preference[12]. However, regularity is followed in the centre bays of all four sides, where it is 6 diameters and in the small bays of the two long sides where it is 2 diameters.

57 Similarly, in the courtyard elevation, some relationship between the Tuscan diameter and the other elements is apparent. The base of the Tuscan column is a ½ diameter, the shaft 6½ and the collar and capital are 45 minutes (1 diameter = 60 minutes); below in the Rusticated order, the cornice and entablature are 1¼ diameters; the column capital is a ½ diameter and each of the rusticated blocks and base block are 1 diameter apiece. In the arcaded basement beneath, the cornice and archivolt are both ½ diameters and the distance from the cornice to the head of the impost is 4 diameters, the impost is a ½ diameter and the pier 4½ diameters. In this apparent relationship of the column diameter to the dimensions of the elevation, Halifax could again be following classical usage, a usage clearly illustrated

12. William Chambers writes in his 'A Treatise on Civil Architecture . . .', 1759, "Among the Antiques, there are no remains of a regular Tuscan Order; the doctrine of Vitruvius upon that subject is obscure; and the profiles of Palladio, Scamozzi, Serlio, Delorme and Vignola are all more or less imperfect."

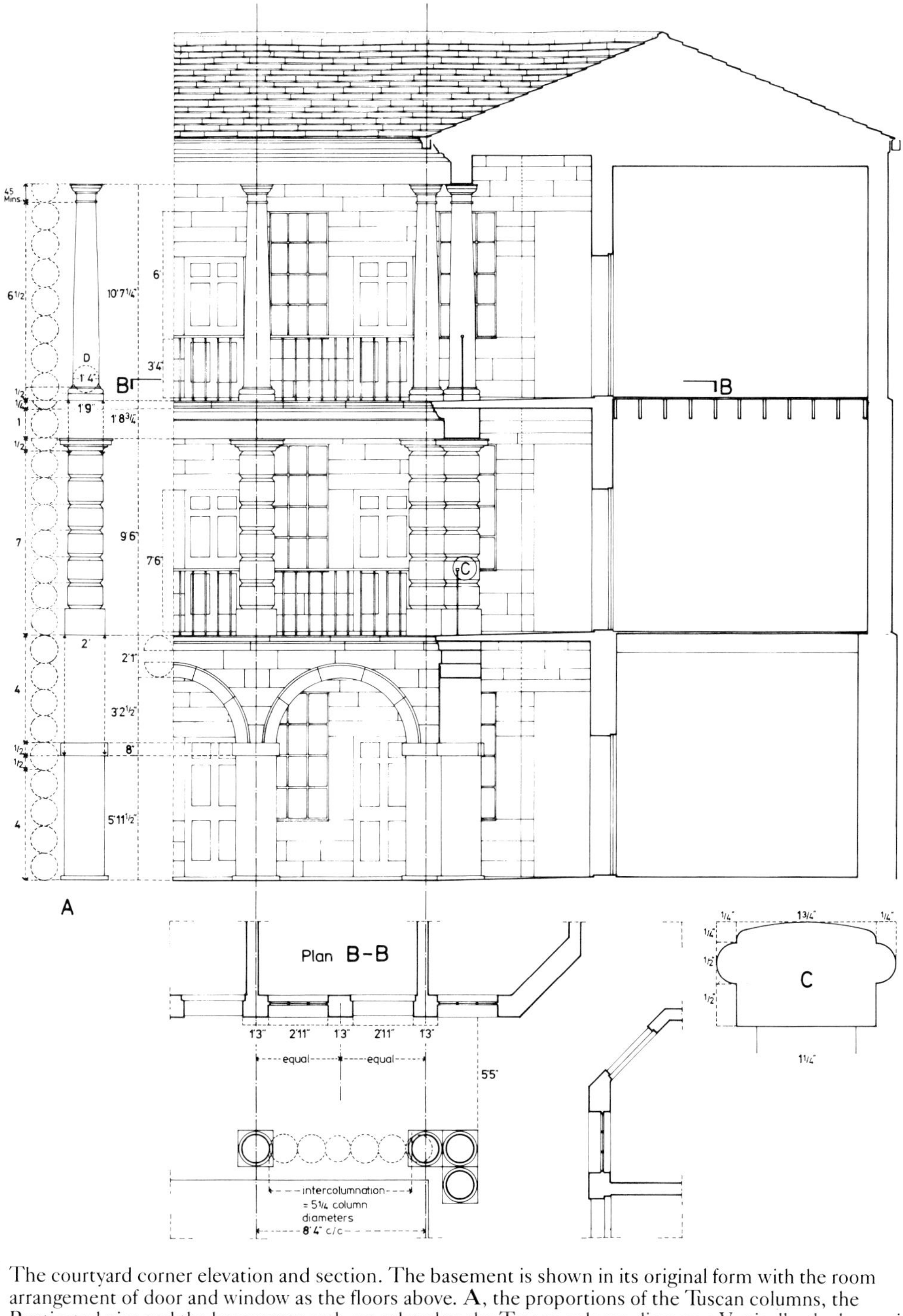

57 The courtyard corner elevation and section. The basement is shown in its original form with the room arrangement of door and window as the floors above. **A**, the proportions of the Tuscan columns, the Rusticated pier and the basements arch are related to the Tuscan column diameter. Vertically, the base widths of each of these elements corresponds to the element beneath. **Plan B-B**, the column spacing (5 ¼ diameters) is centred on the divisions of the rooms behind. **C**, the section of the cast-iron handrail resembles one William Pain illustrates for a staircase, **85**.

by the modular notation in Palladio's Piazze elevation and particularly plainly in Alberti's (Leoni's) detailed elevation where a modular scale appears at the right hand side of the drawing.

Whether this apparent modular correlation in the Hall has any proportional significance – or is intended to – is doubtful. Though the overall size of the courtyard has a definite proportion, it is easy to
54 demonstrate that since the modular spacing of the columns varies between 5¼, 6 and 2 diameters, no proportional meaning is possible. The same is true for the elevation of the courtyard. However, since no practical reason compelled differing heights in the three gallery levels, the marked variation does suggest some proportional treatment is present, but whether this is part of a system, harmonic or otherwise, or is purely arbitrary, is not clear.

For example, if, in a similar manner to the total measurements of the courtyard, the overall
57 dimensions of each level are taken from the foot of each order to the head of each entablature then some tantalising ratios do emerge. All share a common intercolumnation width of 100″ which gives rise to the following proportions for the Tuscan and Rusticated orders: 100″:149″ and 100″:124″. If one inch is allowed to be added to each height then 'perfect' ratios of 2:3 and 4:5 are achieved[13]. However, in the basement no such correlation is found. There, the ratio of 100″:143″ is not close to a 'simple' proportion at all.

As with the basement, if the overall height of the courtyard elevation is taken at its greatest on the lower, three-levelled east side, 416″, and at its least on the upper, two-levelled west side, 273″, the combinations of these with the ideal width, 2760″, and length, 3450″, of the courtyard produce nothing meaningful. For example, 2760″: 416″ = 6.63: 1; 3450″: 416″ = 8.29: 1; 2760″: 273″ = 10.11: 1 and 3450″: 273″ = 12.63: 1.

Some small latitude in correspondence of 'perfect' ratios with marginally 'imperfect' actual measurements can, I think, be allowed. After all, measurement of Palladio's buildings has revealed that often the proportions are significantly at variance with those given for them in the ideal drawings of his 'Four Books'[14]. But, of course, Palladio has told us what he was doing whereas with the Piece Hall, no original material survives to illuminate the intentions of its designers and there is a consequent danger of interpreting into the building meanings never intended. In the case of the courtyard elevation, the upper levels make it tempting to believe a pattern of consistent proportional treatment may exist throughout but the clear discordance of the basement and lack of relationship between the full elevation heights with the courtyard width and length make this very dubious. Whether another system was employed is equally doubtful. The only probable candidate would be the 'Golden Section' but application of its
55 56 principles in plan and elevation reveal little concordance. It is just as possible, and perhaps more credible that no system is present and the heights of the three levels and the total height of the elevation have been decided by simple preference of the designers.

Nevertheless, it cannot be disputed that the proportion of 4:5, intended or not, is there in the courtyard, so what are we to make of it? Though the complete harmonic system is hard to grasp, at least the general courtyard proportions of Palladio and Alberti's 'Piazze' are apparently uncomplicated and quite explicit. If Bradley, or the Hopes, did refer to them, then perhaps they accommodated these obvious ratios to the specific requirements of their courtyard and omitted the full deployment of the system through lack of understanding. If this interpretation is correct, then it would fit well with what we know of Bradley, the Hopes, and as will become clear, the imperfect consistency of the Hall's architectural composition. However, this is only my interpretation of the meaning of the courtyard proportion. Without some firm contemporary evidence of the designer's intentions any attempt to discover what it actually means must have more of the quality of argument than fact. Despite all that has been said of the Renaissance and its influence, it is cautionary to remember that there may be no deliberate meaning at all. In expressing the proportion of 4:5, the Piece Hall may simply be exhibiting the common attribute of architects to have tidy minds.

13. Similarly, when one inch is added to the standard window and door openings, then whole proportions of 1:2 (35″ + 1″:72″) and 2:5 (35″ + 1″:90″) appear.
14. e.g. Palladio, Chapter 5, Principles of Palladio's Architecture, James Ackerman, 1977.

Pattern Books

Similar difficulties are also to be found with the character and origin of the constituent parts of the
Hall which are in many respects not strictly 'correct'. A major difficulty in assessing just how unusual the
Piece Hall details are lies in establishing what 'correct' classicism is. In studying many classical examples
it seems that classicism, even within a particular art historical movement, is far from being a fixed and
rigid system (as many English 18th century architectural books seem to have been trying to make it).
Instead, it appears capable of wide interpretation by each and every architect who cared to work with it.
If there are norms then they are of a general nature, not a specific one: but even in this, the Piece Hall is
close to the boundaries of general norms and on its own in many specifics. In comparison with a 'classic'
arrangement such as the Colosseum the detailed composition of the Hall is, at first glance, more or less *68*
conventional. There are arches on the ground floor, piers on the second and columns on the third.
However, we should note that the sophisticated integration of column/pilaster and arch, repeated on
each level but with successively 'superior' orders of column (Roman Doric, Ionic, Corinthian and
Composite) imposed in the Colosseum and Renaissance buildings, is not present in the Piece Hall.
Here, an arch is an arch, a pier a pier and a column a column, no more and no less. Though in this it does
somewhat resemble the 'pure' ordered columns of both Alberti's (Leoni) and Palladio's Piazze, the richer
detail of theirs is completely absent in Halifax. In this light the Hall can be seen as a highly conscious
reductive classicism or conversely, a blinkered, undeveloped one. More plausibly, the mixture of 'correct'
elements and general design with irregular details and unusual composition, suggest a middling
interpretation.

The main entrance has a number of eccentricities; the first floor crashes through the double height *31*
arch so blocking the upper part off; the gate height corresponds to the interior levels of the Rusticated *61*
gallery and Tuscan colonnade but this is not sufficient to reach the ground on the exterior and extra
blocks have to be employed beneath the pedestals; within the great court the presence of the gate is
barely detectable since the only acknowledgements are a widening of the intercolumnation by *34*
threequarters of a diameter to 6 and the omission of a room at ground level; externally the gate has a
quite different background of smooth sandstone to distinguish it from the rough blocks surrounding the
decorative blank arcading that covers the remainder of the facade – nor is there an architectural link of *58*
either rhythm or detail between gate and arcade.

On entering the courtyard it is striking how the main, longitudinal axis of the North Gate finds no
perceivable expression at all whereas the, secondary cross-axis of the courtyard (where there was *35*
originally no West Gate) not only has a change of rhythm but a doubling of columns as well. The
courtyard elevation itself is unusual in employing the Tuscan column at the highest level. Normally it *67*
would be found at the bottom with the Ionic and Corinthian orders superimposed above. Equally it is
odd not to find a Rusticated order at ground level – though if the building is read as being only two main *32*
levels, the Rusticated and Tuscan column galleries, then it is at ground level on the western side; that is,
the basement arches are merely a below-ground 'foundation'.

Of all the elements within the courtyard itself the Rusticated order is especially odd. Where a *37*
conventional rusticated column would have a clearly recognisable order for its capital and base, in the
Piece Hall the capital is quite alien to the conventional orders and this peculiarity extends to the obscure
forms of the entablature over it.

Where do these details come from? Are they special to the Piece Hall, inventions of its designers,
or, since all parts of the building, however unusual, are clearly or distantly classical, have they a common
source? Though we know of Bradley's Crownest, being a house, it is so different from the Piece Hall that *10 11 12*
it is of small assistance in clarifying the issue. The most important quality this assured but modest
English Palladian design shares with the Hall is the common inspiration of classical Italy. Apart from this
no other original drawing or building by Bradley or the Hopes survives and so, since we know so little of
the work of all three, assessment of their individual responsibility is not really possible which leaves
research in the architectural literature of the 18th century as the sole avenue of pursuit.

58 The north elevation blank arcading and Tuscan North Gate. The arcading is pure decoration in relief, much like the Leeds Third White Cloth Hall. The arcading archivolt, **A**, differs from Batty Langley's **B**, **74**, only in its drip bead moulding. **D**, the arcading has the same radius and springs at the same level as the main gate arch but there is no common rhythm between them or similarity of profile.

If, as seen earlier, there were many books of architectural theory, there were many more of a practical kind, intended for the architect, the gentleman amateur and the builder. They are eponymously characterised as 'pattern books' since they provided fully proportioned and annotated drawings and details for the whole classical vocabulary (and occasionally Gothic), from the five column orders to fireplaces and clocks that enabled an easy reproduction by the reader. Unfortunately, research of the books is handicapped by the lack of a general study to help as a guide.

Mr Charles Hind at the British Museum, who has done some work on them, told me that it was usual for architects and builders to use several different books and choose freely from them. He indicated that the most popular were by Batty Langley, William Halfpenny and Isaac Ware.

Most helpful, however, is John Summerson's book 'Georgian London' which contains an extremely useful short summary of the background of pattern books:

> *"Books were the most important single factor in establishing the dictatorship of Palladian taste throughout the building world. The great period of book production for craftsmen begins in 1715 when two important works were launched. One of these was the first volume of 'Vitruvius Britannicus', a magnificent record of the best classical buildings so far erected in England. The other was a sumptuous edition of Palladio, brought out in instalments by the Italian, Giacomo Leoni. In the Vitruvius the list of subscribers contains the names of several masons, carpenters and joiners, though its aim was clearly to inform and please a much loftier region of society. Within ten years of the event, however, an avalanche had begun of books compiled by craftsmen and exclusively for craftsmen, with a view to instructing them in that self-improvement which would see them on the right side of the fence. I cannot indicate the spirit in which these books were written better than by quoting from the first paragraph of a book called 'The City and Country Builder's and Workman's Treasury of Designs, or the Art of Drawing and Working the Ornamental Parts of Architecture'. It runs:*
>
> > *'The great pleasure that builders and workmen of all kinds have of late years taken in the study of Architecture; and the great advantages that have accrued to those, for whom they have been employed; by having their works executed in a much neater and more magnificent manner than was ever done in this Kingdom before; has been the real Motive that induced me, to the compiling of this work, for their further improvement'.*
>
> *That was written in 1741, but it refers to a process which had been going on for some time . . .*
>
> *The bibliography of the building craftsman's pattern book is enormous. I will only mention some of the more famous and prolific authors. William Halfpenny, a Twickenham carpenter, was responsible, from 1722 onwards, for a continuous stream of books of designs addressed sometimes to the gentry, sometimes to the trade. Batty Langley, a carpenter-surveyor-architect, whose bumptious personality crops up continually on the architectural scene, published, from 1726, over twenty books all containing good, workmanlike plates. Then there were Francis Price, William Pain, Abraham Swan, William Salmon, John Crunden, and later in the century, Peter Nicholson. The main output was between 1725 and 1760; it diminished with the expansion of the architectural profession and the coincident repression of the craftsman's initiative. In the latter part of the century we get a very different wave of book-publishing, sponsored not by craftsmen but by architects, and designed not to instruct the workman, but to charm the potential client.*
>
> *The larger and more academic books, such as 'Vitruvius Britannicus' were usually published by subscription. Books for tradesmen, however, seem to have made tolerably good business for the booksellers, since they were able to put them on the market at anything from 3s. for an octavo book to £1 for a folio. One of Langleys' quarto 'Treasuries' with 184 elaborate and accurately engraved plates, was sold by Harding, of St Martin's Lane, at 16s. (in sheets); it has a subscription list of over 300 names, almost all tradesmen. Halfpenny's useful 'Magnum in Pario', a practical quarto hard book on the orders, cost only 4s., a sum within the reach of every craftsman.*
>
> *Books were the instrument with which the Palladian group unconsciously established its dictatorship, a dictatorship whose rule lasted for thirty years. It is an easy matter to distinguish a*

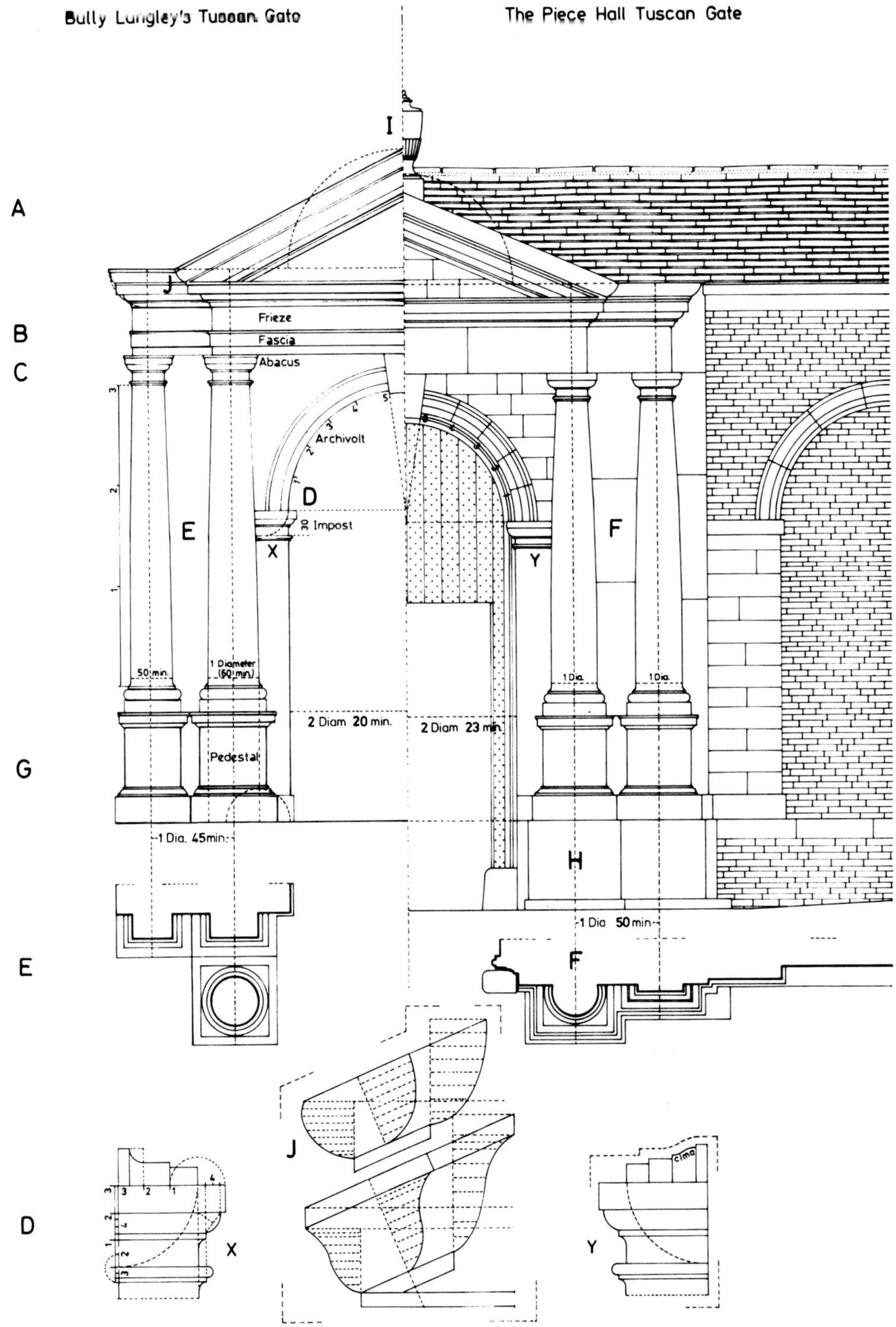

59 The Tuscan North Gate, right, compared with Batty Langley's Tuscan Gate, left, **74**. **A**, the pediment; **B**, the entablature; **C**, the column capitals; **D**, the arch imposts and archivolts; **E**, Langley's free-standing column and attached pilaster; **F**, the Piece Hall three quarter column and attached pilaster; **G**, the pedestals; **H**, the Piece Hall extra bases and **I**, the urn. **J**, Langley's alternative curved pediment profile, the ovolo, **82**, has been substituted for the cima profile shown on his Tuscan Gate, **74**, to assist in the comparison with Halifax.

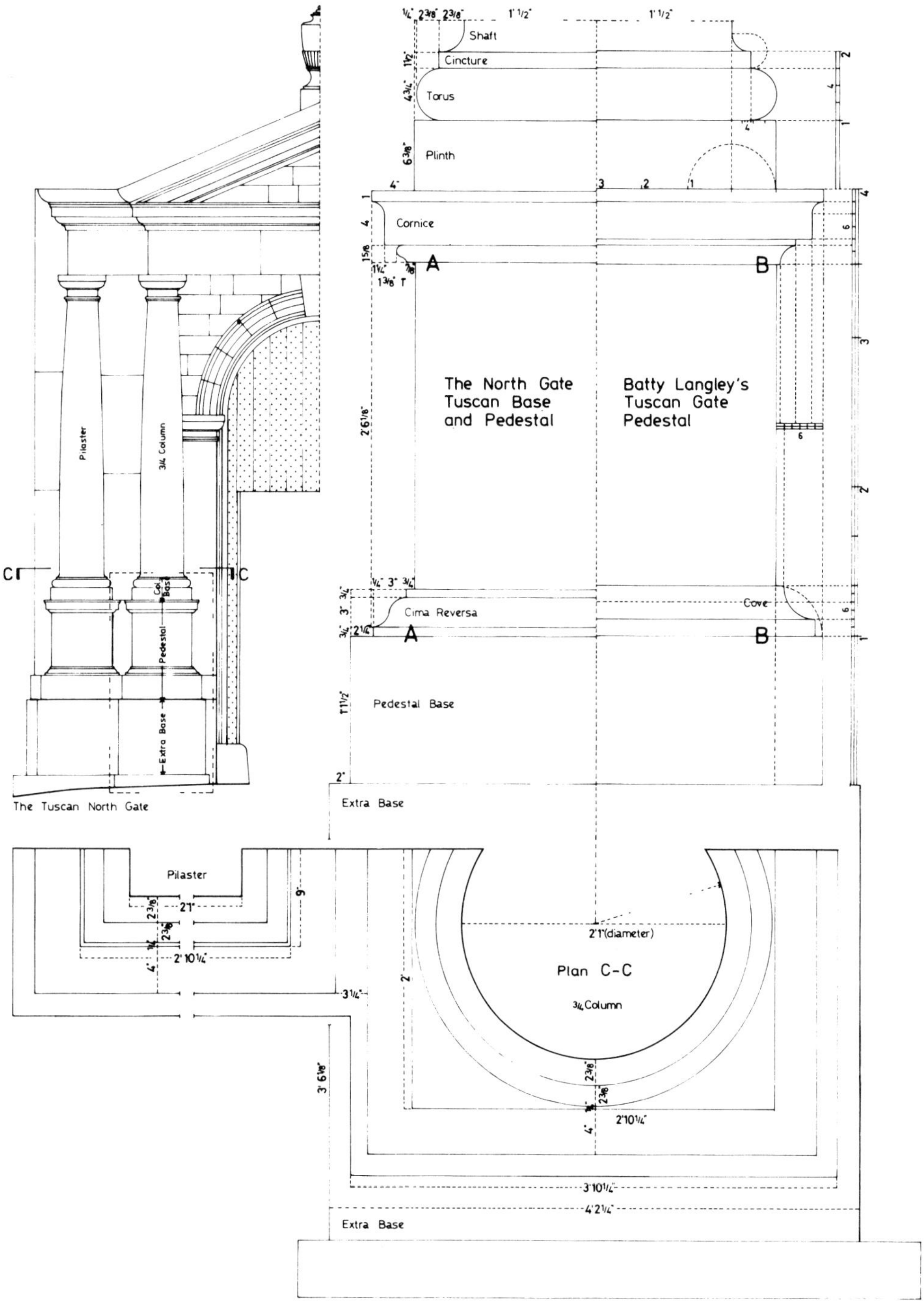

60 The Tuscan North Gate base and pedestal, left, compared with Langley's pedestal, right, **80**. The overall proportions are very similar. The Piece Hall uses cima profiles, **A**, rather than the coves shown by Langley, **B**. Strangely, Langley's use of coves here, contradicts his Tuscan Gate, **74**, where he uses cima profiles.

house of 1715 from one of 1730. But it takes a far more skilled eye to draw distinctions between one of this latter date and one built even as late as 1760. Such was the stabilising influence of the Palladian formula in the copy-book."

Clearly the careers of Bradley, from joiner to architect, and that of the Hopes from bricklayers, to stonemasons, to builders and finally to architects, correspond with Summerson's description of pattern books and their authors very closely. Research in the available pattern books[15] of the period prior to the erection of the Hall for the prototypes of its architectural parts using measured drawings of the Piece Hall elements, details and profiles found some success. One of the most rewarding (as highlighted by Summerson) was Batty Langley's 'The City and Country Builder's and Workman's Treasury of Designs; or the Art of Drawing and Working the Ornamental Parts of Architecture', 1741, 1750 and 1756. Another was William Pain's, 'The Builder's Companion and Workman's General Assistant', 1762. Where similar details and profiles were found, I have drawn them alongside the particular Piece Hall element for ease of comparison. The exact location of each detail or part has been keyed on the general plan and
50 51 elevations of the building for cross referring. The following commentary is to be read in conjunction with each drawing.

59 In detail and general design the Piece Hall gate is strikingly similar to the Tuscan gate contained in
74 Batty Langley's '. . . Treasury of Designs . . .' though there are notable differences. Comparison of the
60 pedestals typifies the problems since they are uncannily close in proportion but vary in profile – a
80 variation which is paralleled in Langley's book between his detailed drawing and that of the entire gate. Most obviously different are the extra bases required to lift the whole Piece Hall gate to the roofline. To maintain the proportions of Langley's gate without extra bases would have increased the gate width so interfering with the column and room spacings of the interior courtyard.

On the face of the Piece Hall gate the threequarter column and pilaster standing on the pedestals are attached to the wall and share identical diameters. Langley's column is free standing and its pilaster is narrower. His column capitals have corona profile abacuses (as the interior courtyard Tuscan columns) but the Piece Hall's are plain.

The gate arch imposts are identical and the archivolts differ only in the use of the Cima profile in the Piece Hall – a profile more usually found in Doric archivolts. Above, the Piece Hall entablature is bare whereas Langley employs the conventional frieze, tenia and fascia. The profiles and pediments are alike though Langley's pediment angle derives from the arch below whereas the Halifax example does not appear to do this. The urn crowning the composition at Halifax is missing from Langley. It is the type of ornament belonging more to the 1770's than the style of the gate and may be a particular
15 contribution of the Hopes who used a similar urn in their funerary memorial to John Caygill.

Besides similarity with Langley there are other reasons to suppose that the gate is not original to Halifax. The Gate does not really tie in to the Piece Hall design as a whole. The way in which the interior first floor passes through the gateway arch and has to be camouflaged by a different material, studded timber, is crude (though effective). If the Gate design were an original, the designer would surely have accommodated this difficulty in a more satisfactory manner.

61 34 And looking at the gate in plan, section and internal courtyard elevation, it is striking how little effect the external Tuscan Gate has on the interior; it is barely detectable. The interior gate intercolumnation is 6 diameters, that is threequarters of a diameter wider than the standard courtyard spacing (it was classical convention to widen the gate spacings slightly) but this is visually hardly noticeable. If the gate opening had been the full clear arch height as the Tuscan Gate design demands, the opening would have been architecturally stated, and visually obvious, but the upper floor would have been interrupted and stairs would have been necessary for access. As it is, pressure for as many rooms as possible, took precedence over design.

The conclusion of these points must be that there are sufficient differences to prevent the assumption that Langley's pattern gate is the prototype for Halifax. However, it is clear both from its similarity to Langley and its detailed lack of integration with the surrounding architecture of the Piece

15. See bibliography 'Pattern Books'

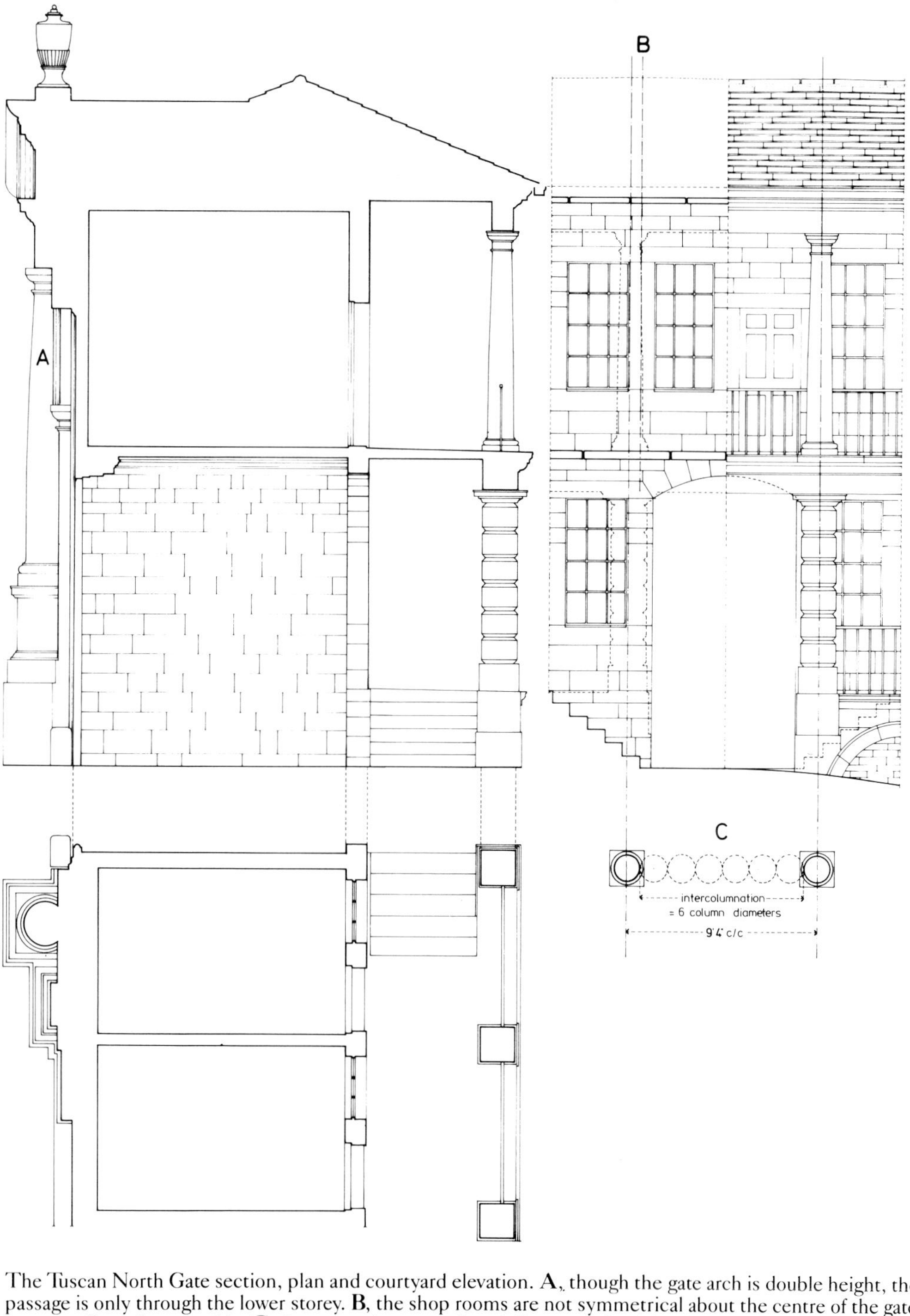

61 The Tuscan North Gate section, plan and courtyard elevation. **A**, though the gate arch is double height, the passage is only through the lower storey. **B**, the shop rooms are not symmetrical about the centre of the gate but are reflected to one side. **C**, the gate column spacing, 6 diameters, is wider than the standard courtyard intercolumnation of 5¼ diameters.

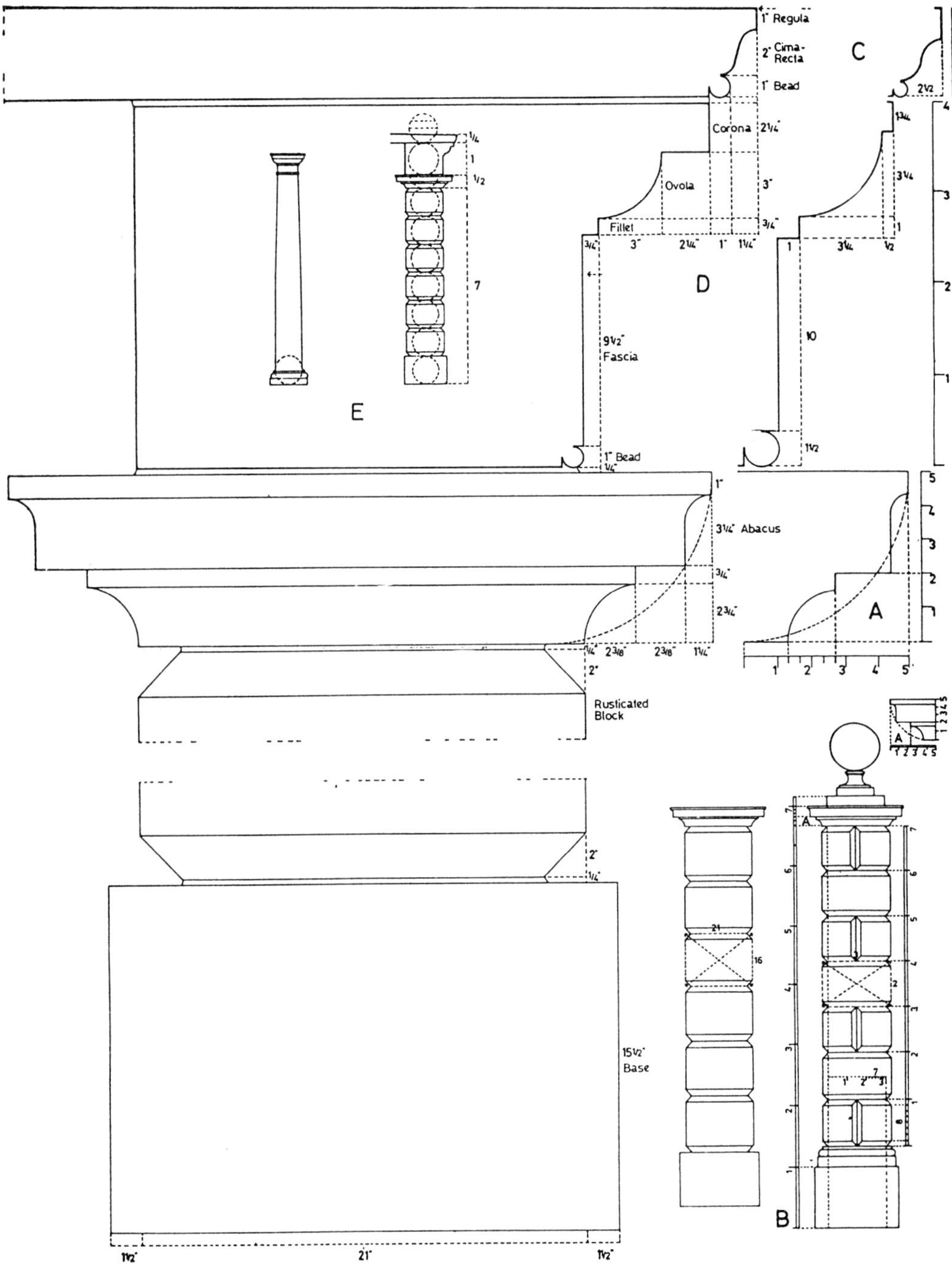

62 The Rusticated pier, compared with Batty Langley's rusticated gate pier, **71**. **A**, the capital of Langley's rusticated gate pier is identical to the Piece Hall and, **B**, the rest of the pier is similar though there are differences of proportion and detail. **C**, the upper part of the cornice, and the lower, **D**, resemble chimney profiles illustrated by William Pain, **83** and **84**, respectively. **E**, the proportions of each part of the pier can be expressed in terms of the Tuscan column diameter.

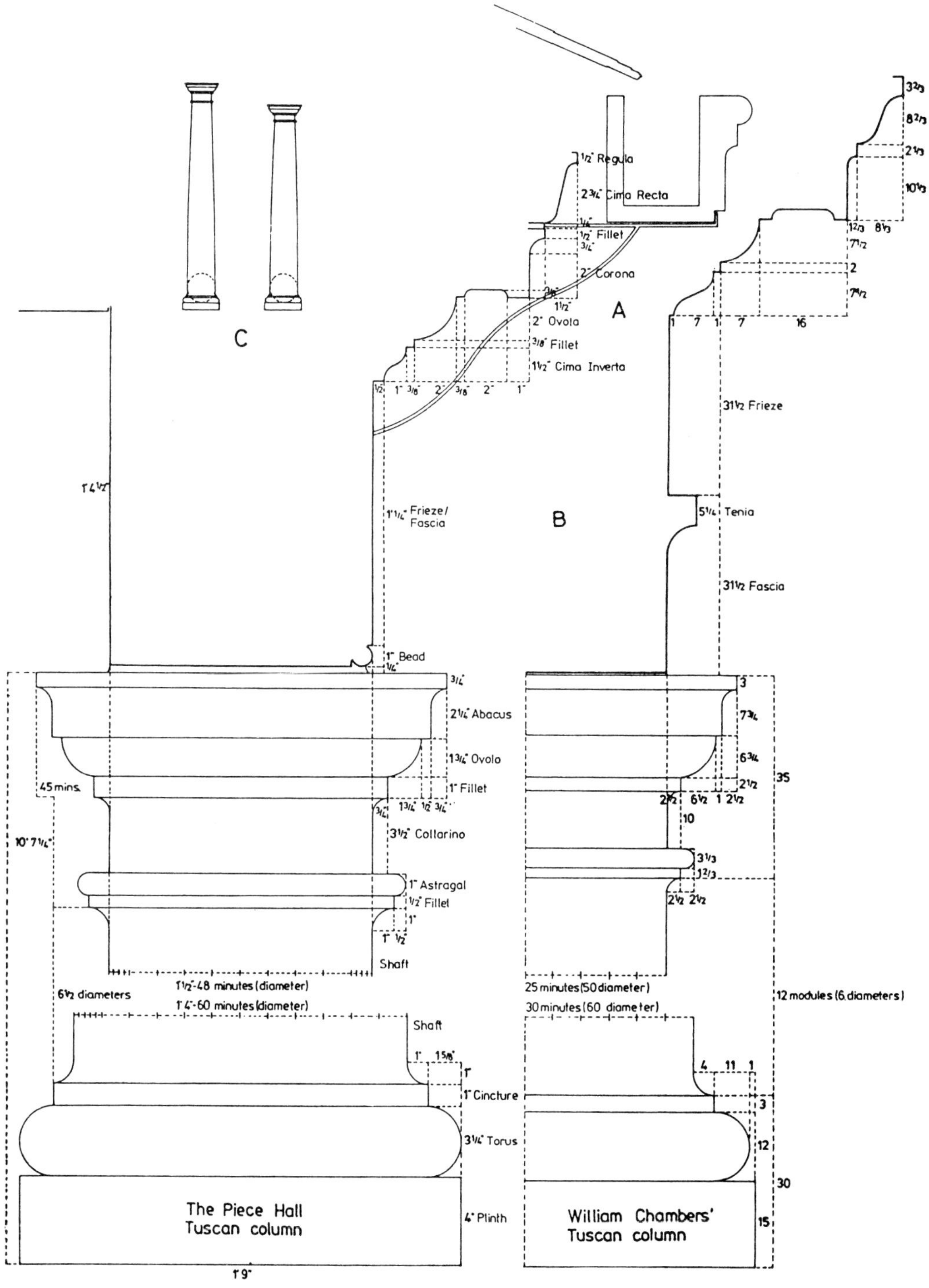

63 The Piece Hall Tuscan column, left, compared with William Chambers', right, 69. **A**, the cornices are identical in profile. **B**, the Piece Hall has no tenia to differentiate the frieze and fascia of the entablature. **C**, proportionally, the Piece Hall column, left, is taller than Chambers', right.

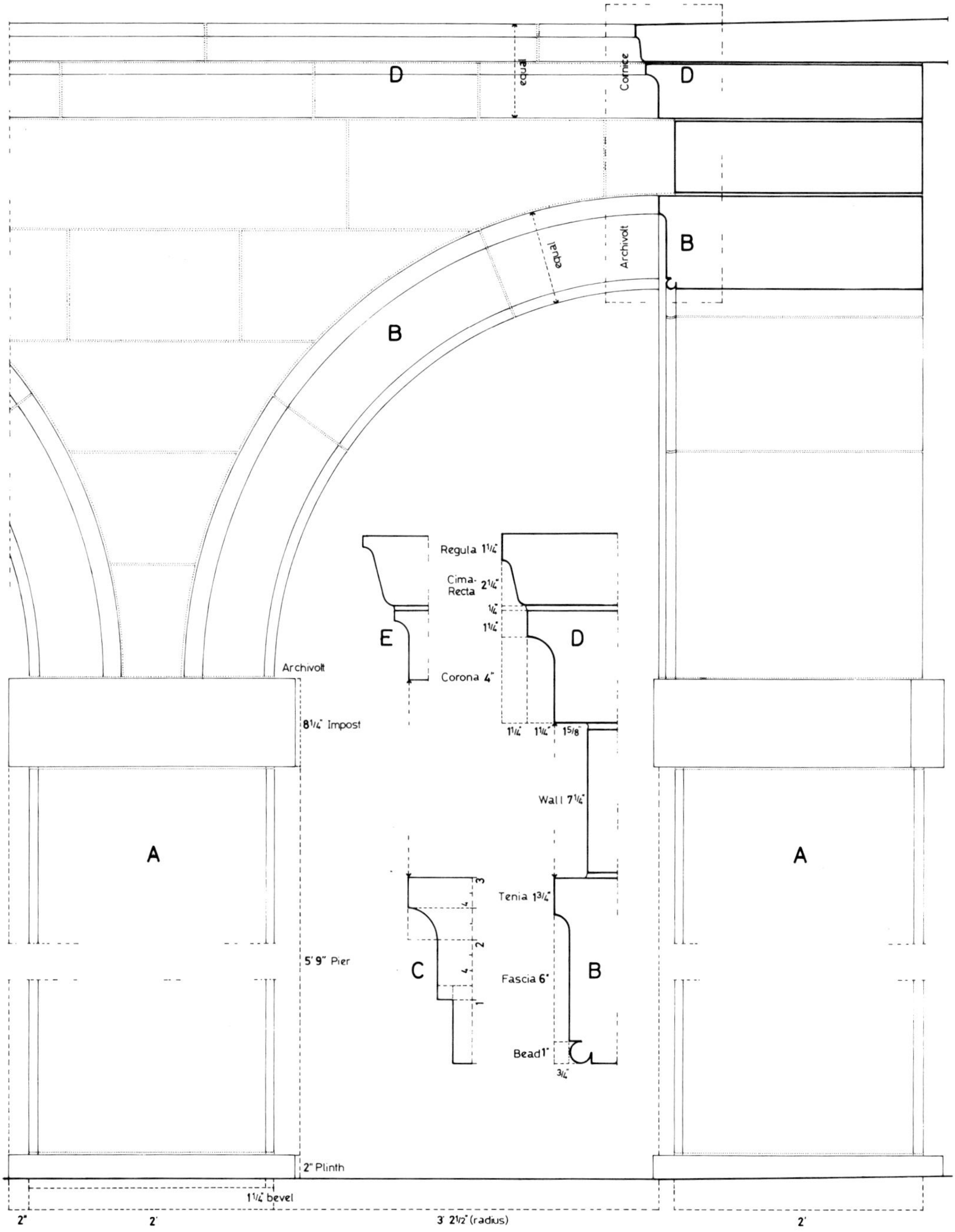

64 The Tuscan arch. The elements of the arch seem to be simplifications of the Tuscan order. **A**, the pier and impost are plain. **B**, the Piece Hall archivolt resembles Langley's, **C**, **74**, but is unique in its use of a bead moulding. The lower half of the cornice mouldings are absent; the profile of the remaining upper part, **D**, is like the Piece Hall Tuscan cornice, **E**, but is much larger (9″) as a proportion of the overall height of the arcade and seems to be related to the adjacent archivolt (8¾″).

Hall, that it is not an original design but has been taken from some source, modified with extra pedestals and a neo-classical urn and placed on the north elevation as an appropriately impressive entrance to the Hall and attractive feature to Caygill's Square.

The other element that has a possible origin in Langley's '. . . Treasury of Designs . . .' is the *62*
Rusticated column. Langley illustrated five gate post designs one of which is very like the Piece Hall *71*
Rusticated column. The profiles of the rusticated blocks are similar though the Piece Hall does not split alternate blocks into two parts, nor does it employ a plinth, torus and cincture above the base block as Langley's design. The capitals are identical but being a gate post, Langley of course, provides no entablature. However William Pain's 'The Builder's Companion' contains profiles very like those of the
Rusticated column entablature on page 64 'Cornice and Architrave Mouldings for Chimneys' and page *84*
66 'Two Cornices for Chimneys at large . . .' – though proportions do not agree. If they are the *83*
prototypes then the column has an entablature formed from internal chimney details!

The Tuscan order in the top gallery is largely correct and similar columns are found in almost all *39 63*
pattern books. Compared with William Chambers' Tuscan column the profiles are much the same *69*
though some proportions differ. The main dissimilarity is, as with the Tuscan North Gate, the omission of the conventional tenia separating the beam into frieze and fascia in the entablature. At the bottom angle of the beam is a bead which acts as a drip; this is an unusual feature. Strictly speaking it is an internal joinery detail and can be found in pattern books of the time. It is used extensively in the Piece Hall on beams and arches.

The remaining elements of the Hall cannot be located in books. The basement arch seems to be *64*
Tuscan since its profiles appear to come from the stable of Tuscan cornices and archivolts found in the Piece Hall. The arch impost and pier are quite plain; the cornice resembles the upper part of the Tuscan column cornice but if this is so then it is only a fragmentary cornice.

The West Gate has no precedent in pattern books or other buildings and must be a design peculiar *33 35*
to the Piece Hall, more of the 1770's in its simplicity than the Tuscan Gateway, but less handsome. The *65*
basic form of the gate comes from the existing internal arrangement of columns, that is a 6 diameter *66*
central bay, flanked by two, 2 diameter bays; this results in the arched gate opening being the full bay and flanking part bays, wide. The stair was probably added at the same time to allow more convenient access to and from the upper Tuscan gallery. As with the North Tuscan Gate, the upper Tuscan gallery crosses the double height arched opening and is lined with studded boarding to differentiate itself from the surrounding gateway stonework. The profile of the archivolt resembles the Tuscan Gate archivolt but it is much wider. The impost is unlike anything else in the building or seen in the pattern books. The blank monolithic pilasters that appear to support the arch imposts and mass of stonework above, are unadorned; their spacing seems to correspond to the interior courtyard intercolumnation. Above them set in ashlar stonework are two large blocks with rough faces that are as wide as the space between the monolithic pilasters below. They are purely decorative relief of the dressed stone. Above the dressed stone is a pediment formed from austere profiles that resemble the cornice section of the courtyard basement arcade. The plain tympanum is relieved by a single blank circular window of profile similar to those in the courtyard central bay. Atop the whole composition is a timber bell cupola tipped by a weather vane incorporating a hung sheep, symbol of the Piece Hall's business and cause of the town's wealth. Internally, the West Gate, like the North Gate, does not impinge on the architecture of the courtyard at all. A low flattened arch (very like that of the North Gate) carries the room wall of the Tuscan gallery above, but that is all that happens. The only sign of the gate is the omission of the ground floor rooms.

The interior 6 diameter central bay opening of the West Gate and flanking 2 diameter bays are
mirrored on the opposite side of the courtyard. Behind the column screen, the room pattern plan is *67*
reflected about the central axis. In the wall above the two arch piers flanking the centre, circular openings are introduced, perhaps as a decorative relief in the wall and perhaps to allow more light to the rooms behind. The profile of the moulding is exactly like the basement arch archivolt; the internal diameter of the opening derives from the space between the two arch piers below, (2 feet).

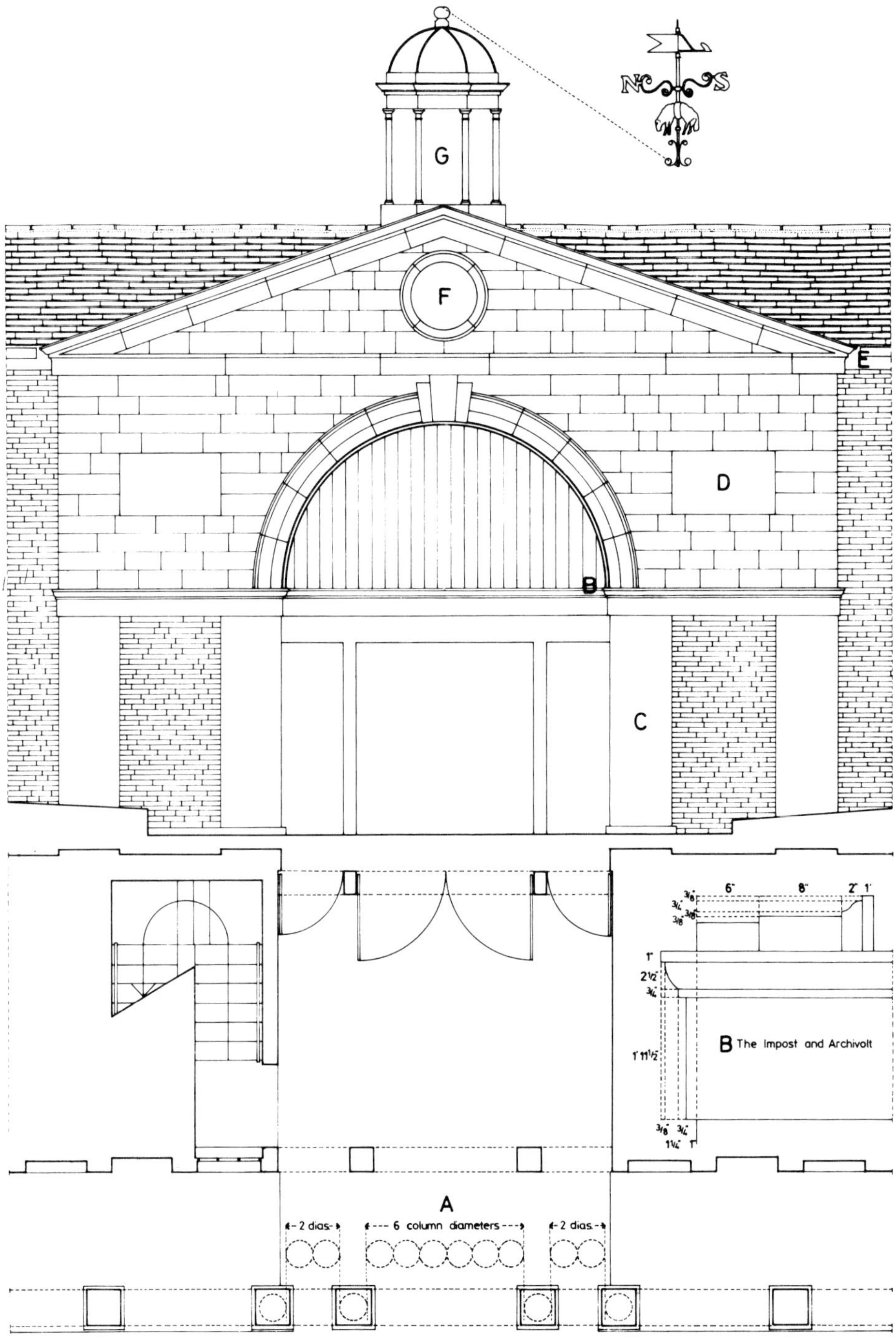

65 The West Gate. **A**, the spacings of the internal courtyard columns; **B**, the arch impost and archivolt; **C**, the pilasters; **D**, rough decorative stonework; **E**, the cornice and pediment; **F**, the circular window and **G**, the bell cupola.

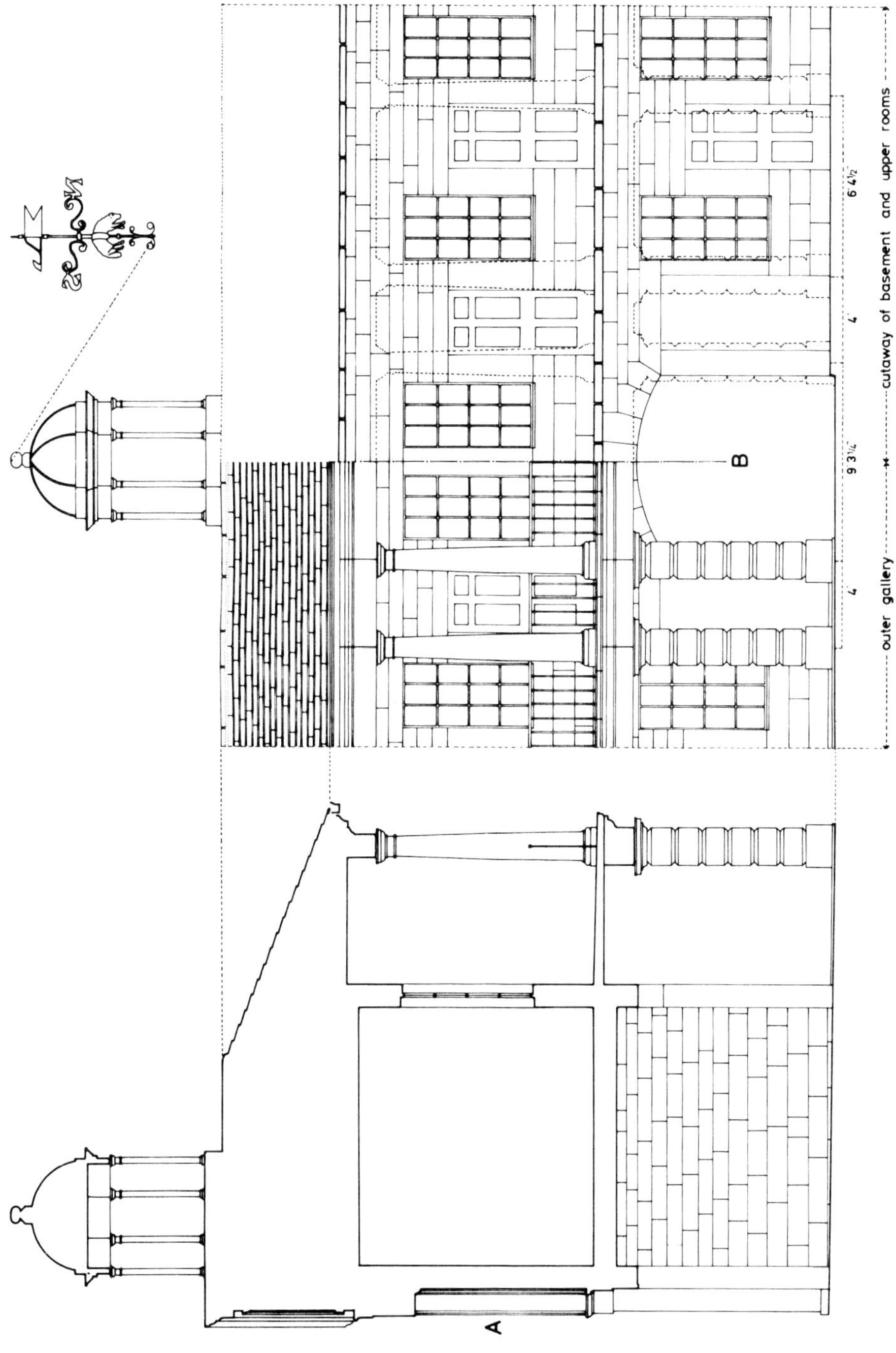

66 The West Gate section and courtyard elevation. Though the gate arch is double height, **A**, the passage is only through the lower storey and the upper rooms continue over. The room arrangement and window and door pattern are symmetrical about the centre of the gate, **B**.

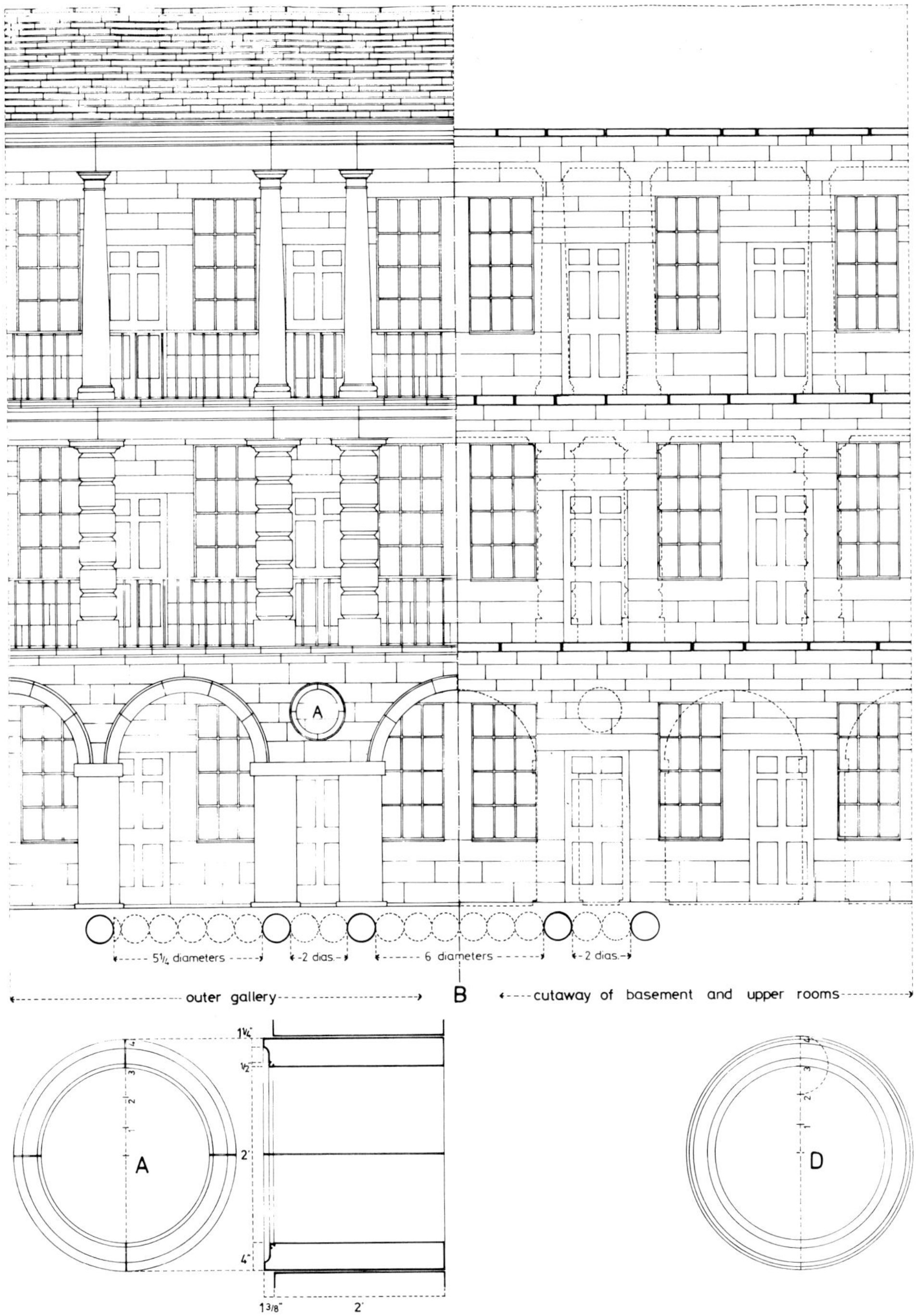

67 The courtyard central bay. The basement is shown in its original form with the room arrangement of door and window as the floors above. **A**, the circular opening has the same proportions as window 'D' illustrated by Langley, **81**, though the mouldings are different. The moulding profile is, in fact, the same as the basement archivolt, **64**. **B**, the room pattern is symmetrical about the centre.

Examined individually, the elements of the Hall appear to have disparate origins but the overall assembly is nevertheless visually coherent and a number of factors achieve this: the predominant use of sandstone for all parts; the prevalent adoption of the Tuscan order for columns and mouldings and most
importantly the purity of the architectural concept of the Hall – a blank walled exterior contrasting with *36*
a completely open, galleried interior formed from the horizontal elements of cornices (lintels) and vertical members of columns (posts). It is a concept that would transcend almost any detailing no matter how curious.

Architectural Language

If we accept the principle that the architectural vocabulary of the Hall originates in the 18th century pattern books of such authors as Langley and Pain, what kind of classicism has been copied and in turn where have they got it from? Though the period falls under the general heading 'English Palladian' a closer look at Langley shows this to be a simplification.

His '. . . Treasury of Designs . . .' is a compilation of many designs, all drawn by Bradley but with no attributions – it is a practical book for craftsmen and builders. However, a much larger work of his, 'Ancient Masonry Both in the Theory and in the Practice . . .', catalogues the full range of classical elements illustrated by the work of many architects, ancient and modern, English and Continental; for example he reproduces the Tuscan orders of the following:

Ancient Roman:	Vitruvius Polio, active 46-30 B.C.	
15th century Italian, Early and High Renaissance:	Alberti	1404 – 1472
	Bramante	1444 – 1514
16th century Italian, Mannerist and Early Baroque:	Giulio Romano	1499 – 1546
	Palladio	1508 – 1580
	Scamozzi	1552 – 1616
	Vignola	1507 – 1573
	Serlio	1475 – 1554
	Michelangelo	1475 – 1564
17th century French Baroque:	Perrault	1613 – 1688
	Le Clerc	1637 – 1714
17th century English Baroque:	Inigo Jones	1573 – 1652
	Wren	1632 – 1723
18th century English Baroque:	James Gibbs	1682 – 1754

This list appears to be typical of the sources of Langley's architectural publications and the designs used bear close comparison with those in the '. . . Treasury of Designs . . .'. The architects are drawn from a period (excluding Vitruvius) covering 300 years, three countries and five distinct classical styles. Though architecturally entwined, the diversity of time, place and style, makes them a collection of mixed pedigrees. Any designer using such a book in a manner unhindered by knowledge, could not avoid creating a hybrid and arguably this is what happened with Bradley and the Hopes at Halifax.

Of all the elements in the Piece Hall, the Tuscan column has the purest lineage and would have *39*
been familiar even to Vitruvius. As we have seen, apart from the absence of a tenia to separate frieze and fascia in the entablature, the Piece Hall Tuscan column is indistinguishable in profile from that illustrated
by William Chambers in his 'Treatise on Civil Architecture . . .' 1759. Chambers' commentary made *69*
criticisms of Tuscan columns by previous architects but acknowledged that his design chiefly imitated Vignola.

"Among the Antiques, there are no remains of a regular Tuscan order; the doctrine of Vitruvius upon that subject is obscure; and the profiles of Palladio, Scamozzi, Serlio, Delorme and Vignola, are all, more or less, imperfect.

Of the two designs left us by Palladio, that taken from the description of Vitruvius, is unpleasingly rustic. The other again is too rich, and injudiciously composed. That of Scamozzi is yet richer, and too much like the Doric. Serlio's is heavy; and Vignola's though superior to the others, is defective in the cornice, which is clumsy compared with the rest of the order, ill proportioned in its parts, and incorrectly profiled, as it finishes with a supporting moulding, which has nothing to support, and, consequently must excite the idea of a mutilation; the more striking, as the general outline of the composition, resembles exactly the bed moulds of the Ionic cornice; supposing the dentil band left uncut, as is often the case.

In the design here annexed, I have chiefly imitated Vignola's, who in this order has been almost universally followed."

Who Vignola copied is not immediately significant, the point being that the Piece Hall column belongs to an almost timeless line of classical usage.

37 The Rusticated column that stands beneath it is completely the opposite; it is unique. Its distinctive feature, rustication, though, is not. John Summerson, in 'The Classical Language of Architecture' explains its history:

"... I cannot begin to talk of Giulio (Romano) without explaining the meaning of a word of great significance in classical architecture from this time on (c.1520) – rustication. What is rustication? As the word rather implies, it was first conceived to mean a rough countrified way of laying stones, each particular stone retaining some of the individuality it had when hewn from the quarry. However, this rustic roughness was recognised as having character – artistic possibilities – and it became, in due course, the subject of extreme sophistication. Already, by the time Serlio was writing his fourth book (published 1537) rustication had been stylised and systematised. From being just rough it had become highly artificial – cut into geometrical facets. Serlio describes rustication, however, as being fundamentally a mixture of the natural and the artificial – he seems to imply a sort of struggle between the artificer and the forces of nature. This, of course, is a thoroughly romantic idea and in the works of Giulio Romano we can see it at work ... Giulio didn't invent rustication (the Romans used it; Brunelleschi used it; Bramante had used it in the House of Raphael), but Giulio did bring it to a pitch of expressiveness which no one else had dreamed of and from which very few architects after his time failed to benefit ... The long-term effect of Giulio's inventions was tremendous. Even Palladio, who you might think would be proof against such explosive stuff, borrowed from him in his later palaces. In eighteenth century England, Newgate Prison had Giulio to thank for its horrific solemnity."

As Italian Mannerism developed into Italian Baroque, so rustication developed and became part of any architect's – and certainly of all the architects reproduced in Langley's books – classical
71 vocabulary. Langley's gate posts can be traced from this body of Baroque amd Mannerist forms and in
70 turn the Piece Hall rusticated column has its parentage there too. But in the inventive spirit of Giulio Romano (albeit unconscious), the column is a very free design; it could have been altered in many ways and we would have been none the wiser.

The use of rusticated piers in Halifax was not limited to the Piece Hall. Intriguingly they featured in
3 some Halifax houses of the period immediately prior to its erection, as in the example of Stansfield, Lower Ashes, a hill farm remodelled about 1759. Doubtless they too came from pattern books and perhaps were influential in their appearance in the Piece Hall.

32 If the Rusticated column is unique then the basement arch is obscure. Such an austere design does not appear in Langley's works or any other pattern book which only show arches with fully articulated
72 imposts and elaborate archivolts for even the plainest Tuscan arches. Similar arches occur in Palladio and
73 the buildings of Vanbrugh but pattern books do not reproduce the work of the latter, perhaps because the English Palladian movement (to which the pattern books are central) is a reaction to his Baroque

68

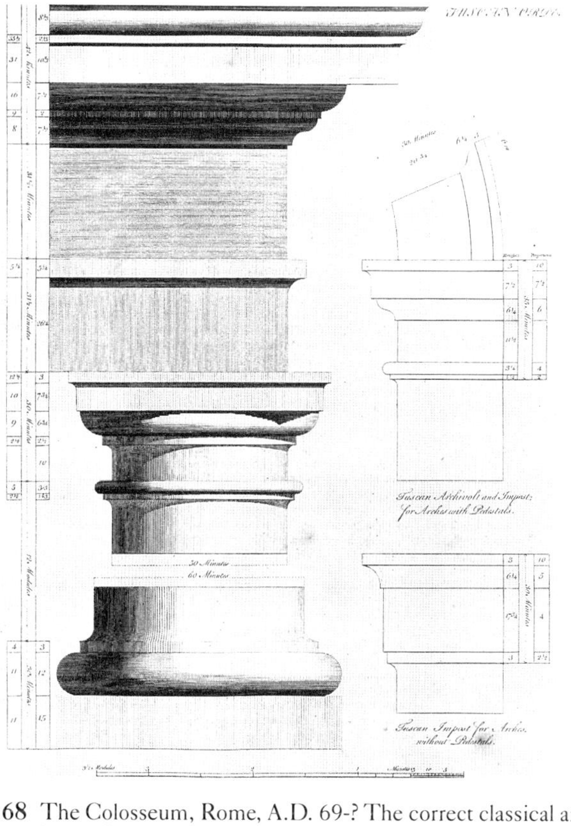

69

70

68 The Colosseum, Rome, A.D. 69-? The correct classical arrangement of superimposed orders: Roman Doric, Ionic, Corinthian and on top, Composite. It is a sophisticated integration of attached column and arcade.
69 The Tuscan order from William Chambers' 'A Treatise on Civil Architecture . . .', 1759.
70 A rusticated Tuscan pilaster from Vasari and Vignola's Mannerist Villa Papa Giulia, Rome, 1550-55.

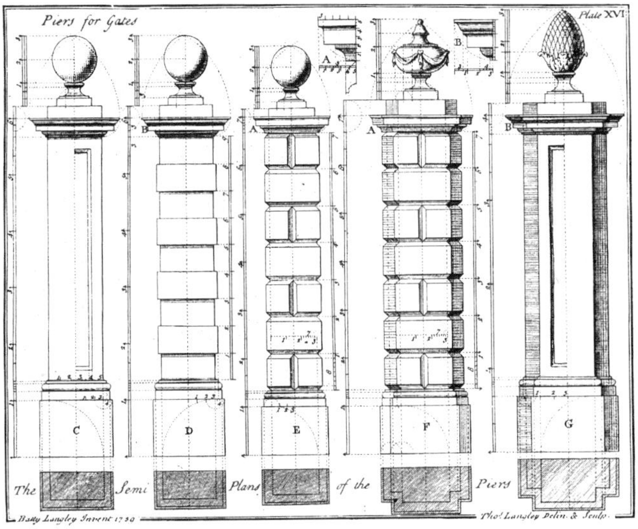

71 'Piers for Gates' from Batty Langley's '. . . Treasury of Designs. . .', 1740, Plate XVI. Pier 'E' is very similar to the Piece Hall rusticated column and the capital 'A' is identical.

72 The arcade of Palladio's Villa Emo, c.1560; the simplicity of the arch pier, impost and archivolt is reminiscent of the Piece Hall basement arcade.

73 Eastbury north wing, Vanbrugh, c.1724-38. The plain Tuscan arcade resembles the Piece Hall's.

74 

 75

76 

 77

74 The Tuscan Gate from Langley's '. . . Treasury of Designs . . .', 1740, Plate XXI.
75 The facade of Palladio's Il Redentore, Venice, 1577, with the correct spacing between column and pilaster.
76 Vignola's Church of the Gesù, Rome, 1568; the flanking pilasters abut the columns around the central door.
77 Detail of the end pavilion of Palladio's Triumphal Bridge from the 'Third Book' Plate X; an example of a full arch framed by a pediment and columns.

style. Where Bradley or the Hopes might have come across him is not clear. Without more definite information, speculation on the stylistic source is all that is possible.

31 Fortunately study of the Tuscan Gate is more rewarding. Though the components of both
74 Langley's gate and the North Gate are Palladian and it would be natural to think of both as Palladian compositions, this would not be strictly true. Palladio never assembled them in this particular way, his pedimented gateways being far more archaeologically correct. Nor is the design found in ancient Roman or Italian Renaissance architecture.

59 The secret of its origin lies in its form. The gates' constituent parts are a pediment carried on two Tuscan columns standing on pedestals, a cornice and entablature carried on flanking Tuscan pilasters and a central arch springing on Tuscan imposts. Each assembly stands in its own plane, the pedimented columns are at the front, in the middle lies the cornice, entablature and pilasters and behind comes the Tuscan arch and imposts. Conceptually, all three have been telescoped together to form a layered design. And in elevation it can be seen that the flanking pilasters abut the Tuscan columns with no intercolumnation between; they have been drawn together to form a compact design.

Such a layered composition in plan and elevation typifies Mannerist-Baroque architecture. One of Langley's source architects, Vignola, employed the arrangement of a central pediment and columns in
76 front of abutting flanking pilasters and entablature in the facade of the Church of the Gesù, 1568. In
75 Palladio's classical facade of Il Redentore there is no similar telescoping or compaction, it is a far more archaeologically and rationally correct composition. Palladio did, however, use a full height arch between and within the framework of columns and pediment, (for instance in the end pavilions of his unbuilt
77 Triumphal Bridge). The combination of this with Vignola would give the complete arrangement of the Piece Hall Tuscan gate.[16]

Theory

If the Hall is a mixture of forms derived from the Romans, the Renaissance, Mannerism and the Baroque, it is one further complicated by irregular details and the omission of standard parts. It certainly does not form a stylistic unity. Nevertheless, viewed collectively the building would naturally be seen as firmly in the English Palladian camp. It is of that movement's time (just) and its architecture is mirrored in whole and part in its literature. But with the exception of local histories it was never published in architectural books of the 18th or the 19th century, whereas, of course, Bradley's Crownest House appeared in the New Vitruvius Britannicus. If it was an English Palladian building, then it was one not taken to its heart.

Why such an impressive composition should be so neglected is a puzzling question. Palladian purists must have disliked its combination of eccentric and incorrect details. But more than this, they would have judged the fall across the courtyard unforgiveable and have felt keenly the lack of Palladian
47 48 proportions. For the Piece Hall to achieve ones similar to Palladio's Roman Piazza the plan would have to be reduced to a quarter of its actual size whilst retaining the full height of the courtyard elevation.

From the earlier discussion of the proliferation of theoretical and practical texts in 18th century England, it will have become apparent that this represented an almost breathless effort to assimilate and catch up with European architectural development. The Piece Hall can be seen as a material compendium of this process. But the conflict between the Hall's English Palladian intentions and the quantity of accommodation required resulted in a building as much of the future as it was of the past. For the modular repetition of so many identical rooms and elements leaves Palladianism and the 18th century sensibility of propriety and scale behind and becomes instead a harbinger of 19th century
78 industrial architecture. Seventy years later, in the Crossley mills of Dean Clough in Halifax, the

16. The influence of Batty Langley's '. . . Treasury of Designs . . .' endured far beyond its own time. The original 1740 edition of the '. . . Treasury of Designs . . .' currently in the RIBA Library belonged first to Gertrude Jekyll and then Sir Edwin Lutyens.

78

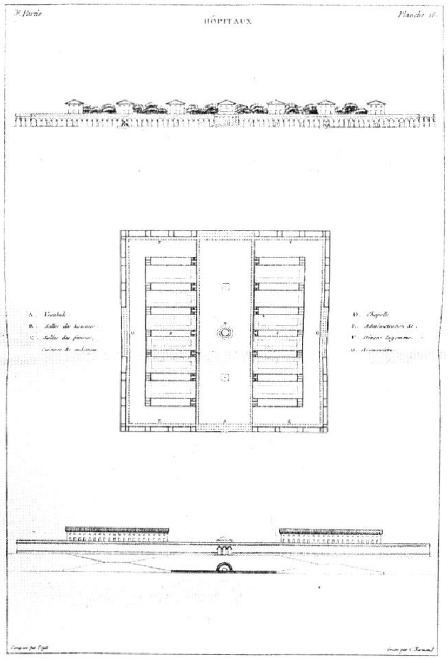

79

80
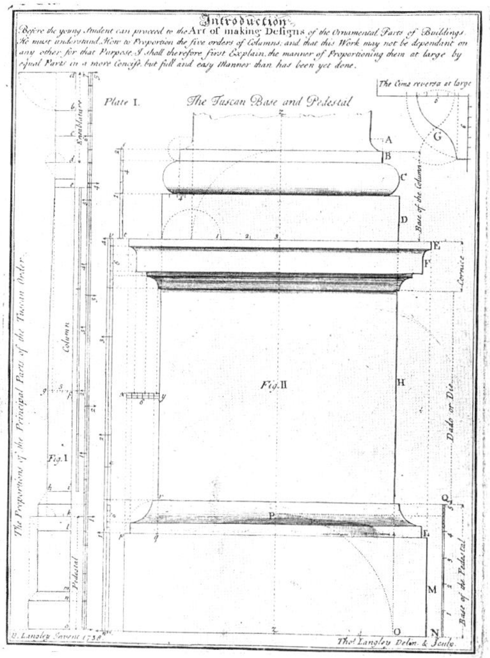

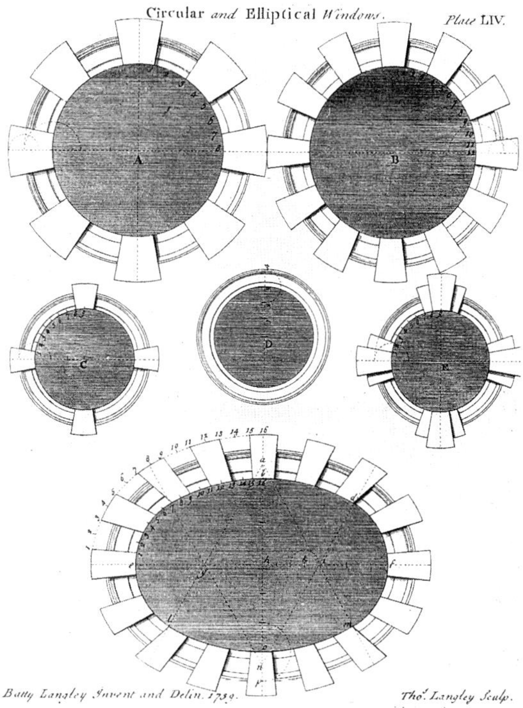

81

78 The Crossley carpet mills at Dean Clough, Halifax, about 1850; a purely functional architecture. Behind rises the spire of Gilbert Scott's All Souls, Haley Hill.
79 J. N. L. Durand, design for a hospital from 'Précis . . . II', 1809. The large scale and modular repetition of parts are akin to the Piece Hall.
80 The 'Tuscan Base and Pedestal' from Langley's '. . . Treasury of Designs . . .', 1740, Plate I.
81 'Circular and Elliptical Windows' from Langley's '. . . Treasury of Designs . . .', 1740. Plate LIV.

adornment of graceful architecture had been discarded to leave only the plain stone wall and the endless repeated windows that lie behind the columned galleries of the Piece Hall[17].

If, in this way, the Hall is something of a pivot between the architecture of the 18th century and the 19th, then we can see at the point of balance, a reflection of the contemporary, rational theory of the Abbé Laugier published in his 'Essai sur l'Architecture' in 1753. John Summerson in 'The Classical Language of Architecture', writes of this:

"... and it was left for ... the Jesuit Laugier, nearly fifty years later, to announce a theory which really did upset the architectural apple-cart and shift the basis of architectural thought for a century to come. Perhaps more than a century; because I am not sure that Laugier may not justly be called the first modern architectural philosopher.

Now the established hypothesis of all architectural theorists was that architecture had originated when primitive man built himself a primitive hut. From the hut he went on to the temple and, refining continually on the temple formula, he invented the timber version of the Doric order and then copied it in stone. The other orders followed. That was the the theory and everybody accepted it. But what nobody had done was to think at all concretely about the primitive hut; and this is what Laugier did. He visualised it as a structure consisting of upright posts, cross beams and a pitched roof ... This, he declared, was the ultimate image of architectural truth, 'the model' (to use his own words) 'upon which all the magnificences of architecture have been imagined'.

Here, for the first time, the basis of authority of the orders was undermined – displaced by something else, by an image of their own hypothetical prototype, which is functional, a rational prototype. Not that Laugier wanted to banish the orders: on the contrary, he believed that further orders might be invented. But he wanted architects to use them with the same sense of constructional truth as the posts and beams in the primitive hut. He agreed with Cordemoy that all 'architecture in relief' must go, but he went further in wanting even walls to go. For Laugier, the ideal building consisted entirely of columns – columns carrying beams, carrying a roof.

... Anyway, in 1753, no architect could have proposed anything so crazy as the abolition of walls. But Laugier was not an architect; he was a philosopher and he was dealing in abstractions. He knew, of course, that walls could not be and would not be abolished, but he was establishing a principle of architectural beauty and that principle, he believed, had been revealed to him as quite necessarily an affair of columns. And it is not at all difficult to be with him in this. Look. A single column is just – well, a point on a plan; or rather a very small circle on a plan – it gives you the module of an order but nothing more. But two columns give you at once an intercolumnation, therefore a rhythm and there, with the module, you have the germ of the whole building ... (my underlining)

But what effect did Laugier's book, his 'Essai sur l'Architecture', have in 1753? In France it was devoured; in England and in Germany translations appeared within two years. It was discussed and attacked, digested or rejected all over Europe. In actual building terms it is fair to say that any fresh, innovating work after about 1755 is certain either to be coloured by Laugier's views or to show a positive rejection of them."

And of course Laugier's thoughts and an illustration of the primitive hut were reproduced in Chambers' 'Treatise on Civil Architecture' in 1759, a treatise available to the designers of the Piece Hall as a source for their Tuscan column.

36 38 The Piece Hall is a building of blank external walls, without windows and with the exception of the
north elevation, without articulation. Within, the courtyard is quite the opposite. Formed by an open
32 grid of assembled elements, the horizontals are created by the stone cornice floor edges and the verticals
by columns and piers. Apart from the arches, it is a screen of posts and lintels which the simplified
cornices and profiles complement and emphasise. (Though the arches are clearly assembled elements

17. The Hall equally represents an economic and social hinge. For the Piece Hall gathered within one place, for a few hours each week, the disparate, self employed efforts of many men working in a cottage industry, to market their collective 'mass' production. By 1810, the cottage industry had been eclipsed by the industrial mills and those individual piece makers were gathered under one roof as employed workers in centralised mass-production.

of the screen and are fully part of the courtyard 'lining'.) In this manner, the Piece Hall does tantalisingly follow many of Laugier's precepts. There are no pilasters, no 'architecture in relief'; there is an invented 'order' – the rusticated column; the columns and cornices are used truthfully – the columns bear the load and the cornices literally are the floor slabs. There are walls behind, but the courtyard itself is a pure 'affair of columns' related in their intercolumnations and heights by the diameter of the Tuscan order. The Piece Hall Tuscan column can be seen as the 'module' of the courtyard – 'the germ of the whole building'.

And looking beyond Laugier, a purely literary theorist, to a 19th century disciple, J. N. L. Durand, who reflected a severe rationalism derived from Laugier, both in his writing and designs, a similarity of scale and repetition in his projects can be seen to the Piece Hall. This is not to suggest that Bradley and *79*
the Hopes were architectural revolutionaries unbeknown to their contemporaries, posterity and themselves. There is no concrete reason to suppose that they were any more than a young, inexperienced local man and ambitious mason-builders, all aspiring in their careers to be architects. But it is undeniable that something of the pure spirit of Laugier is there in the Piece Hall design though perhaps it is forced on the building by the accommodation requirements of the brief and not learnt from books. But then the rationalism of Laugier and Durand and the architectural austerity it entailed is paralleled in the economic rationalism of the industrial architecture of the mills and the spartan buildings that produced. The former arises from a concept of truth and beauty, the latter more from an awareness of cost and necessity.

Lessons

Any building, however modest or grand, is, in some degree, a mixture of necessity and artifice. As the proportion varies we may recognize architecture or merely see only a building and naturally most are somewhere in-between. In the case of the cloth halls of Leeds, Wakefield and Bradford we might say that the portion of necessity is greater than the measure of artifice. But whatever credence may be given to my arguments for the origin, nature and meaning of the Piece Hall, it is quite clear that here, architecture is predominant.

Yet the Piece Hall cannot really be seen as a building of the front rank. Were the Hall designed by a prestigious architect such as Chambers or a first rate one like Carr, we would expect a greater sophistication of stylistic synthesis in the parts and the whole that formed completely assured relationships throughout the building and with the world outside. That the Hall has these qualities only in part is, though, no failure but rather the occasion of astonishment that they are there at all. The Hall rose in a small town of unassuming architectural tradition, was paid for by manufacturers who lived and worked in the hills and designed by men of scant training with little of our opportunities for education or first hand experience of the rich architectures of the past. If the Hall has deficiencies then they are those of pioneers accomplishing an ambitious goal but, through no fault of their own, lacking the full ability to master all aspects of the enterprise.

In its shortcomings, peculiar inventions and applied archaeology the building belongs to a particular Englishness of architectural design – the Englishness of, for example, St. Paul's Cathedral. My comparison is not meant in terms of aesthetic mastery but in the desire to combine Italian ideas with English tradition. In the example of St. Paul's, it is the combination of the Italian centralised church plan with the traditional longitudinal basilican arrangement of the English Gothic cathedral. The marriage is somewhat incomplete and all sorts of conscious deceptions are used (concealed flying buttresses, decorative arches in the crossing and so on) to make it appear that it is successful. With the Piece Hall the fusion of Italian concept with market hall tradition was far better handled but the discrepancies appear in the assembly of the architectural parts.

Externally, the integration of the Hall with the rest of Halifax gave rise to similar mixed results. Its great size, relative to the town, precluded any attempt at 'fitting-in', which an architect today might feel himself obliged to do (though what it could do it did by completing Caygill's Square), but this in no way mitigated its architectural success. No doubt the quality of materials and the provision of its great

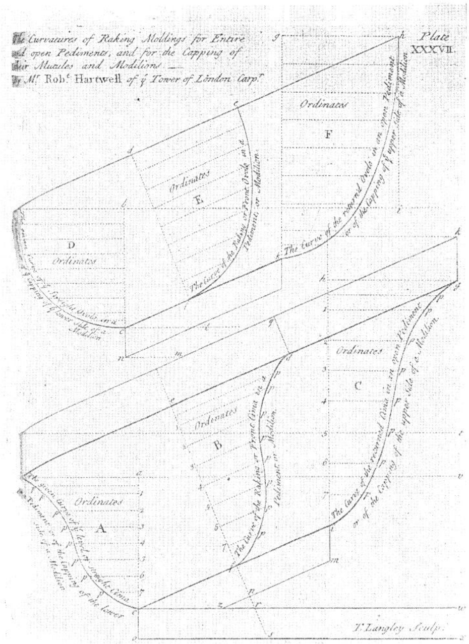

82

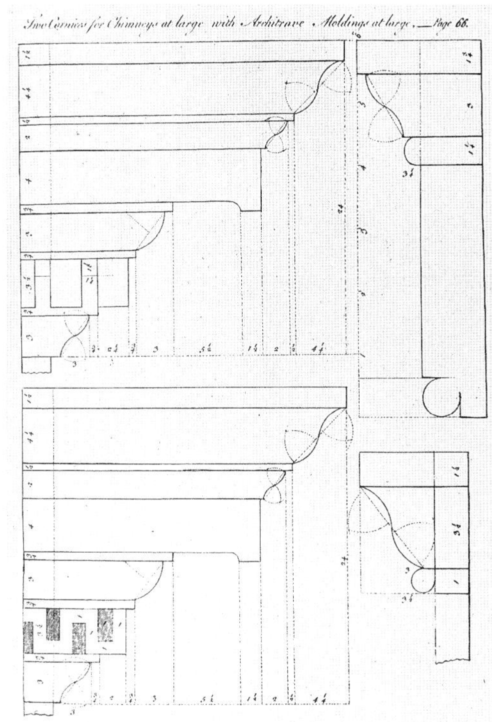

83

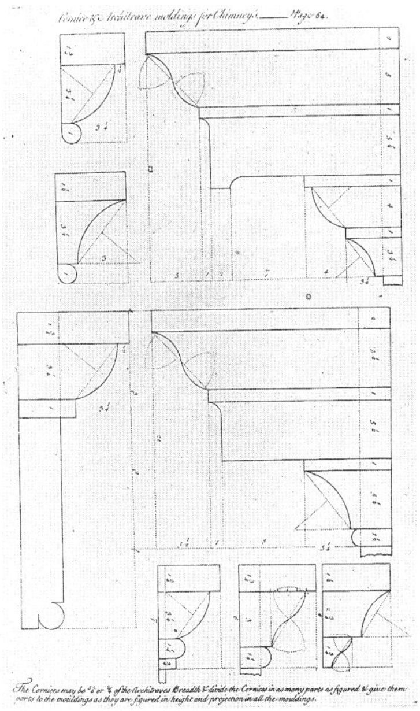

84

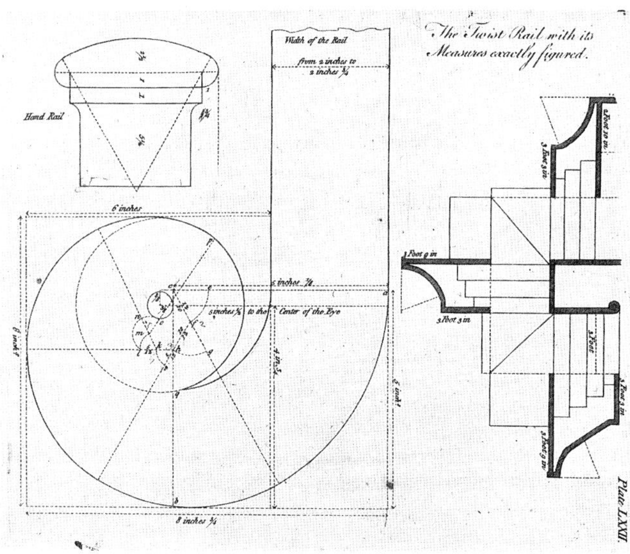

85

82 The Curvatures of Raking Mouldings for Entire and Open Pediments . . . from Batty Langley's 'The City and Country Builders' and Workmans' Treasury of Designs . . .', 1740, Plate XXXVII.
83 'Two Cornices for Chimneys at large with Architrave Mouldings at large', page 66 from William Pain's 'The Builder's Companion and Workmen's General Assistant', 1762.
84 'Cornice & Architrave Mouldings for Chimneys', page 64, from William Pain's 'The Builder's Companion and Workmen's General Assistant', 1762.
85 'The Twist Rail with its Measures exactly figured', from William Pain's 'The Practical Builder, or Workman's General Assistant . . .', 1774, Plate LXXII.

courtyard played their part in this, but surely the contribution of the Hall's wholehearted embrace of classicism cannot be underestimated. In its many reincarnations classicism has proved time and again one of the most durable and beautiful of all architectures. It can hardly be overlooked, and the Piece Hall is a good instance of this, that classicism, in common with other former styles, even when handled uncertainly, is such an attractive language that some measure of success is inevitable. It is a tradition of enormous wealth and depth comprising centuries of sustained achievement providing an almost inexhaustible supply of extraordinary examples to benefit from. By this adoption the companions of the Hall became not merely the adjacent buildings of Halifax or the cloth halls of neighbouring towns but, transcending time, the thoughts of the Renaissance and forums of the Romans. Of course we should not be blind to the fact that there was nothing inevitable about the Hall's appearance. It reflects the primary influences of the period of its construction but, had it been conceived 30 years later, we might have had a Greek Doric hall, or, 100 years more, a Gothic one, without such a change affecting the essentials of its form or, perhaps, our enjoyment of the building. For the Hall embodies a temper of mind at ease with the past, neither subservient nor anarchic, ingenuously re-working tradition for its own original ends.

Though the Hall may be imperfect, it exemplifies a wholly admirable marriage of business and architecture and its estimable qualities stand as a touchstone of achievement for the present, all the more potent an example through its humble origins and the relative anonymity of its creators. The Piece Hall was greeted enthusiastically by the people of Halifax with processions, song and fireworks not purely for the prosperity and prestige it would bring but also for the pleasure its splendour evoked – a splendour whose antiquity, their song made clear, they were well aware of. Today the benifits of the Hall are, if anything, enhanced. For the characteristic of architecture to endure through the years makes it, in a sense, timeless, its effect only increased by the erosions of age and accretions of memory. It matters little if the original use disappears for its nature bestows a separate existence outside of function which continues to exert influence consciously and unconsciously, to those around. The study of such a building is not a concern of solely academic interest but the appreciation of an existing building of architectural merit and considerable urban richness. There are many worthwhile lessons to absorb.

It is our good luck that the Hall has survived the oscillations of architectural thought and the vicissitudes of economic fortune. Happily, it has not been preserved purely as a venerable monument but continues to form part of a working town centre of similarly remarkable aspect. Both are valuable, not only for their inherent quality, but also through the recognition that such a standard of architecture can only be achieved by persistent effort over hundreds of years; it is simply irreplaceable. Such buildings are not old and purposeless structures from another age but rather are the heart of a town and the fabric of its past. Who is there who does not gather around them works of value and permanence and *38*
who would not want the same for our towns and cities?

86

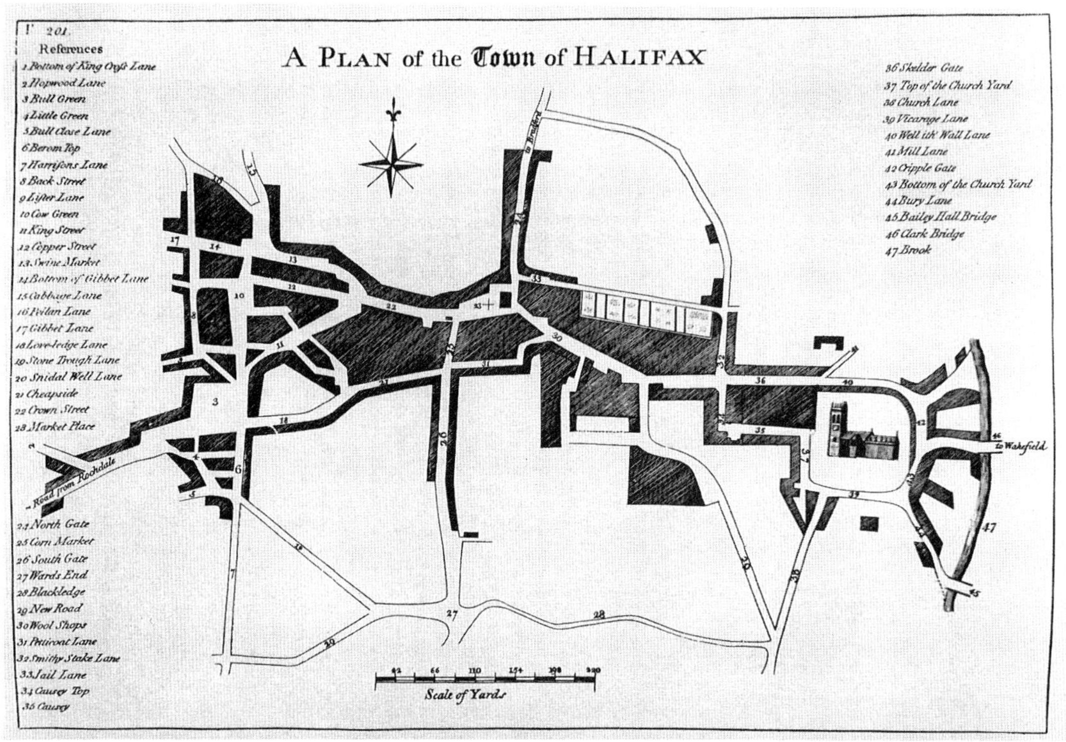

87

86 Pre-1775 plan of Halifax from 'The History and Antiquities of Halifax', Rev. Watson, 1775.
87 Moore's plan of Halifax, 1797.

APPENDIX 1

Articles of Agreement indented made and entered into this tenth day of June one thousand seven hundred and seventy five By and between James Wood William Ackroyd and John Preston all of Halifax, masons of the one part and James Pitchforth of Elland mason and George Anderson of Guisley, mason of the other part as follows to wit:-

Will do perform and execute all the masons work for the South Quarter of the Piece Hall intended to be forthwith erected in the Talbot Field in Halifax At and for the prices and upon the Terms and Conditions stipulated – mentioned in the paper writing hereunto annexed And shall and will execute – finish all such masons work in a workmanlike manner and to the satisfaction of the Architect and Surveyor now appointed or hereafter to be appointed to superintend the building of the said Piece Hall The whole of which work to be finished and compleated within the time the said James Pitchforth and George Anderson are by their Agreement with the Committee of the Subscribers towards erecting the said Piece Hall obliged to finish and complete the same And the same to be certified for by the said Architect and Surveyor In consideration whereof the said James Pitchforth and George Anderson do hereby covenant and agree to and with the said James Wood William Ackroyd and John Preston to pay them for such work so to be performed and executed as aforesaid at and after the several Rates and prices in the same paper writing hereunto annexed mentioned And to pay them such prices monthly as the said work shall be from time to time executed and performed and to find and provide for the said workmen sufficient of suitable and proper stone and also all necessary Scaffolding And for the true performance of these Articles on the parts of the parties thereto respectively to be performed they do hereby bind .. .. oblige themselves each to the other in the penal sum of .. .. one hundred pounds firmly by these presents In Witness whereof the parties have hereunto set the Hand and Seals the Day and Year written.

Signed sealed and delivered (being first duly stamped) in the presence of	James Wood
	William Ackroyd
by all the parties except the within named George Anderson	The Mark of X John Preston
J. Marshall	James Pitchforth

The Paper Writings referred to in and by the annexed ????

	£.	s.	d.
For building the Foundation Wall (of the Dimension James Pitchforth and George Anderson have agreed to build it) per Rood	–	4	–
If broader to be advanced in price in proportion and if narrower to be deducted			
For Wall above the plinth dref'd to the Sample and Dimensions the said James Pitchforth and George Anderson have agreed at the Rood	–	9	–
For all chisel'd Masonry well tool'd in – Rustic Pillars Plinth Impost and faced Courses at the superficial Foot	–	–	4
For Columns with tops and Bases to Same and all Cornices and other moulded – work at the superficial foot	–	–	6
For walling the In Walls Delf dref'd at per Rood	–	7	–
For Ashlar Wall of Great Stone of nine Inches thick getting working and heading and setting included at per Rood exclusive of the Hollows according the said James Pitchforth and George Anderson's Measurement of one yard in Height and seven Yards in length	1	6	0
If thicker to be paid in Proportion for every Doorhead or Task	–	3	–

Halifax Reference Library: reference MISC : 3/72/1/2

ESTIMATE
of the
MANUFACTURERS' HALL AT HALIFAX
by Saml. and John Hope
1775

The following are the particulars of the estimate, omitting those of the North side:-

EAST SIDE	£.	s.	d.
Digging and levelling earth	11	0	0
Foundation walling, etc., 116.58 roods at 12s.6d	72	17	3
Delf dressed walling, 217.147, @14s	152	0	1
Hammer dressed walling 2.22 roods at 18s. 6d	2	1	1
Ashlar wall in arcade storey, 44.23 roods at 46s.8d.	103	4	1
Ashlar wall in principal and colonnade storeys 70.60 roods at 37s.4d	131	15	8½
Add for work to doors and windows as per agreement, 108 rooms at 10s	54	0	0
Corner stones for tooling only, 151ft. 1in. at 3d	1	17	9¼
Soughing the east side	5	10	0
Lime and sand for do	100	0	0
Plain tooled work, 15022 ft. 8in. at 8d	500	15	1¼
To cramp, lead, and labour to frieze joints, 136 at 1s. 3d	8	10	0
To iron hand rail and banisters to stairs steps	20	0	0
To Pillar shafts, 4,393 ft. 4in. at 10½d	192	4	2
Stone mouldings, 5,006ft. 3in. at 1s	250	6	3
Flagging, 5,190 ft. 10in. at 1½d	32	8	10
Brickwork, 283.76 roods at 9s.	127	13	10
Bond timbers to walls, 110 at 2s	11	0	0
Floor framing, 101.50 sq. ft. at 19s	96	8	6
Boarding floors, 89.76 sq. ft. at 22s. 10d	102	9	6
Ceiling joists, 91.64 sq. ft. at 10s	45	16	5
Principal Trusses, 31.44 sq. ft. at 35s	55	0	4¾
Back of roof 87.45 sq. ft. at 21s	91	16	5¼
Slating, 1,058.78 yds. at 1s. 3d	66	3	5½
Lead, 10 yards lineal at 7s. 6d	3	15	0
Wall plaistering, 5,459.5 yards at 6d	136	9	9
Ceiling plaistering, 1,966.55 yds. at 1s	98	6	6½
Doors with hinges, latch, painting etc., 112 at 15s	84	0	0
Sashes, 2,563ft. 3in. at 4¼d	45	7	9¼
Painting, screws, and casements, 108 at 4s. 6d	24	6	0
Do. to cellars, 17 at 2s. 3d	1	18	3
Casements to do. 8 at 1s. 6d	0	12	0
Glass to sash squares, 1,881 ft. 6in. at 11d	86	4	8½
Superintending and contingencies	100	0	0
	£2,815	18	11½
SOUTH SIDE			
Digging and levelling earth	5	10	0
Foundation walling, 109.53 roods at 12s. 6d	68	9	1½
Delf dressed walling, 154.34 roods at 14s	108	0	9
Hammer dressed stone 10.67 roods at 18s. 6d	9	17	4½
Ashlar wall, 15 in. thick, 18.27 roods at 46s. 8d	42	12	7
Ashlar wall, 12in. thick, 56.76 roods at 37s. 4d	105	19	0
Add for work to doors and windows as per agreement, 72 rooms at 10s	36	0	0
Flagging, 3,388 ft. 4in. at 1½d	21	3	6½
Plain tooled work, 8,964 ft. at 8d	298	16	0
To cramping friezes, cramps, lead and labour to joints, 198 ft. at 1s. 3d	6	15	0
To iron handrail and bannisters	11	0	0
To do. to steps out of area	13	0	0
Pillar and shafts, 2,538 ft. at 10½d	111	0	9

continued on page 91

brought forward from page 90

Corner stones for hewing only 82ft. 6in. at 3d	1	0	7½
Stone mouldings, 3,305 ft. 4in. at 1s	165	5	4
Lime and sand for south side	3	10	0
Gates to south entrance, 80ft. at 1s. 6d	6	0	0
Brickwork, 206.56 roods at 9s	92	19	0½
Floor framing, 58.385 at 19s	55	9	3½
Boarding floors, 58.18ft. 4in. at 22s. 10d	66	0	0
Bond timbers to partition walls, 80 at 2s	8	0	0
Principal trusses, 24.99 sq. ft. at 35s	43	14	7½
Back of roof (nails found by committee) 72.24 sq. ft. at 21s	75	17	0½
Slating, 871.19 sq. yds. at 1s. 3d	54	8	11¾
Lead, 10 yards linear at 7s. 6d	3	15	0
Ceiling joists, 67.70 sq. ft. 2 in. at 10s	33	17	0
Doors, with painting, hinges, latch, etc. 72 at 15s	54	0	0
Sashes, 1,740 ft. 4 ins.at 4¼d	30	16	4
Painting do., with screws, casements, etc., 72 at 4s. 6d	16	4	0
Do. with screws, and letting into cellar, 14 at 2s. 3d	1	11	6
Casements to every other of do., 7 at 1s. 6d	0	10	6
Glass, 1,285 ft. 7in. at 11d	58	18	5
Plaistering walls, 3,632.25 yards at 6d	90	16	1½
Ceiling plaistering, 1,055 yards at 1s	52	15	0
Superintending and contingencies	100	0	0
	£1,923	12	11¼

WEST SIDE

Foundation walling, 82.77 roods at 12s. 6d	51	14	7
Delf dressed walling, 108.09 roods at 14s	74	13	3
Ashlar walling, 1ft. thick, 70.56 roods at 37s. 4d	131	14	3
Digging and levelling the earth	12	0	0
For work to doors and windows, 72 rooms at 10s	36	0	0
Plain tooled work, 7,345 ft. 9in. at 8d	244	17	2
To cramping ye friezes, lead, labour and cramps to 136 joints at 1s. 3d	8	10	0
Iron handrail and bannisters to stairs	11	0	0
Corner stones, for hewing only, 82ft. 6in. at 3d	1	0	7½
Pillar shafts, 2,482 ft. 1in. at 10½d	108	11	9¾
Mouldings in stone, 3,105ft. 4in. at 1s	155	5	4
Lime and sand for west side	65	0	0
Soughing	8	10	0
Flagging, 5,554 ft. 4 in. at 1½d	34	14	3½
Brickwork, 191.21 roods at 9s	86	0	10½
Wall plaistering, 3,609 yds. at 6d	90	4	6
Ceiling plaistering, 1,180.44 yds. at 1s	59	0	5½
Bond timbers to ye party walls, 74 at 2s	7	8	0
Ceiling joists, 74.70 sq. ft. at 10s	37	7	0
Floor framing, 40.50 sq. ft. at 19s	38	9	6
Boarding floors, 36.00 sq. ft. at 22s. 10d	41	2	0
Principal trusses, 31.44 sq. ft. at 35s	55	0	4½
Back of roof (nails found by committee) 87.45 sq. ft. at 21s	91	16	5¼
Slating, 1,058.79 sq. yds. at 1s. 3d	66	3	5½
Lead, 10 yards lineal at 7s. 6d	3	15	0
Doors, with painting, hinges, and latche, etc., 72 at 15s	54	0	0
Sashes, sheets, 1,575 ft. at 4¼	27	17	9¾
Painting do. with casements, screws, etc., 72 at 4s. 6d	16	4	0
Glass to sashes, 1,122 ft. at 1d	51	8	6
Superintending and contingencies	100	0	0
	£1,770	9	2¾

	£	s.	d.
Estimate, West Side	1,770	9	2¾
Estimate, North Side (similar particulars)	1,950	17	8
Estimate, East Side	2,815	18	11½
Estimate, South Side	1,923	12	11¼
	£8,460	18	8½

BIBLIOGRAPHY

Chapter One – CLOTH MANUFACTURE AND ORGANISATION
'The Manufacturer's Hall'; two articles by F. A. Leyland; the first published in the Halifax Courier, 9th April, 1887 and the second in the Halifax Guardian 7th May 1887. 'The Halifax Piece Hall'; article by J. S. Roberts published in the 'Yorkshire Architect', No. 58 January/February, 1978. 'The Cloth Industry – Handlooms – Cloth Halls'. Booklet published by the Pennine Heritage Network, 1982. 'The Halifax Piece Hall', R. A. Innes, Metropolitan Borough of Calderdale, 1975. 'A Tour Through the Whole Island of Great Britain', Daniel Defoe, 1724.

Chapter Two – DEVELOPMENT OF THE PIECE HALL DESIGN
'The Story of Old Halifax', 1920 & 1986, T.W. Hanson.The Leeds Mercury newspaper, notices and correspondence 1774-75, Huddersfield Reference Library. 'Piece Hall and Square', R. Bretton, Halifax Antiquarian Society Transactions, 1961. 'The Yorkshire Coiners', Ling Roth, 1906; Halifax Reference Library.

Chapter Three – WHO WAS THE ARCHITECT OF THE PIECE HALL?
'Thomas Bradley master-builder' and 'William Bradley and the building of Coley Church', Reginald Spink, Halifax Evening Courier, 22nd and 29th April 1978. 'Jacob's History of Halifax', 1787; Halifax Reference Library. 'Biographical Dictionary of British Architects', 1954 & 1978, H. Colvin. 'The Halifax Piece Hall', M. Garside, Halifax Antiquarian Society Transactions, 1921. 'The Canals of Yorkshire and North East England', Vol. 1, C. Hadfield. 'Pigot's Directory', 1829, Manchester Reference Library. 'The New Vitruvius Britannicus', G. Richardson, 1802. 'Dictionary of British Sculptors, 1660-1851', R. Gunnis. 1968. 'Gentlemen's Magazine', May 1817, page 568, Manchester Reference Library. 'Manchester Directory, 1772-1804', contained in the Owen MSS, Vol. 34, pp.100-101. Manchester Reference Library. 'Georgian London', John Summerson, 1945 (Century Hutchinson). 'The beginnings of the architectural profession in Scotland', Howard Colvin, Architectural History, Vol. 29: 1986.

Chapter Four – THE CLOTH HALLS OF THE NEIGHBOURING TOWNS
'West Yorkshire Architects and Architecture', 1978, Derek Linstrum. 'History of the Huddersfield Woollen Industry', W. B. Crump and Gertrude Ghorbal, 1935. 'Links with Bygone Leeds', Vol. 52, Thoresby Society, Leeds Reference Library. 'A History of Modern Leeds', Kevin Grody, Leeds Reference Library. 'Records of Leeds Coloured Cloth Hall, 1755-1889', DB 24, Leeds Reference Library. 'The Yorkshire Woollen and Worsted Industries, Chapter II, the Leeds White Cloth Hall', Thoresby Society, H. Heaton, 1931. 'Pen and Pencil Pictures of Old Bradford', Scruton; Bradford Central Library Archive Department. 'The Old History of Bradford', J. Hartley, 1776; Bradford Central Library Archive Department. 'The Tammy Hall at Wakefield', John Goodchild, Wakefield Library.

Chapter Five – ARCHITECTURE
'A History of Building Types', Chapter 15, N. Pevsner, 1976.
'Architectural Principles in the Age of Humanism', R. Wittkower, 1949. 'The Classical Language of Architecture', John Summerson, 1963. 'Essai sur l'Architecture', M. A. Laugier, 1753, Paris. 'Nouveau Traité de Toute l'Architecture', De Cordemoy, 1706. 'Leçons' J. N. L. Durand, Paris, 1801-05.

BOOKS OF THEORY
'De Re Aedificatoria', Leon Battista Alberti, 1485. 'Ten Books on Architecture', English edition, Giacomo Leoni, 1726, London. 'I Quattro Libri dell'Architettura', 1570, Venice. 'The Four Books of Architecture', English edition, Giacomo Leoni, 1715 and Isaac Ware, 1738. 'The Architecture of A. Palladio. . .', Giacomo Leoni, 1715 and 1721, London. 'Designs of Inigo Jones and Others', Isaac Ware, 1735, London. 'Regola delli cinque ordini d'Architettura', Giacomo Barozzi da Vignola, 1562. English editions 'Rules for the Five Orders of Architecture', 1669 and 1702. 'A Treatise on Civil Architecture', Sir William Chambers, 1759, London. 'Vitruvius Britannicus', Colin Campbell, 1717 and 1725, London. 'A Book of Architecture', 1728; 'Rules for Drawing the Several Parts of Architecture', James Gibbs, 1732. 'Works of Architecture with Remarks and some Observations', Sebastian Le Clerc, 1714, Paris; English edition, William Chambers, 1732. 'The Theory and Practice of Architecture: or Vitruvius and Vignola abridg'd..', English translation, Joseph Moxon, 1703. 'Familiar Architecture; consisting of original Designs for Houses for Gentlemen and Tradesmen..', Thomas Rawlins, 1768, London. 'Palladio Londinensis', William Salmon, 1734, London. 'The Mirror of Architecture', Vincenzo Scamozzi, translation W. Fisher, 1669, London. 'A Dissertation Upon the Orders of Columns and their Appendages', John Wood, 1750, London. 'The Ruins of Baalbek', Robert Wood, 1757, London.

PATTERN BOOKS

WILLIAM HALFPENNY
'The Art of Sound Building demonstrated in Geometrical Problems shewing Geometrical Lines for all kinds of arches, niches, groins and twisted rails . . . with several draughts of buildings and staircases'. London, 1725. 'The Country Gentlemen's Pocket Companion and Builders Assistant for Rural Decorative Architecture', 1753. 'A Complete System of Architecture, delineated in a variety of plans – elevations – estimates of each design', 1759. 'A new and complete system of Architecture delineated in a variety of plans and elevations of designs for . . . houses . . . also an estimate of each'. 1749. 'Practical Architecture; or a Sure Guide to the true working according to the rules of that science', 1730.

WILLIAM AND JOHN HALFPENNY
'The Modern Builder's Assistant; or a concise epitome of the whole system of architecture . . . Engraved on eighty-five folio copper plates from the designs of William and John Halfpenny . . . Robert Morris . . . and T. Lightoler', 1757.

BATTY LANGLEY
'Ancient Masonry, both in the Theory and in the Practice . . . Illustrated by . . . examples engraved on . . . copper plates, 2 vols.', 1734. 'The Builder's Chest-Book; or a Compleat Key to the Five Orders of Columns in Architecture', 1727. 'The Builder's Director, or Bench-Mate: being a Pocket-Treasury of the Grecian, Roman and Gothic orders of Architecture . . . Engraved on 184 copper plates', 1746. 'The Builder's Compleat Chest Book . . .', 1738. 'The Builder's and Workman's Treasury of Designs . . .', 1770. 'The City and Country Builder's and Workmen's Treasury of Designs; or the Art of Drawing and Working the Ornamental Parts of Architecture', 1741, RIBA Library.

BATTY AND THOMAS LANGLEY
'The Builder's Jewel: or the Youth's Instructor, and Workman's Remembrancer Explaining short and easy rules . . . for drawing and working', 1746.

ROBERT MORRIS
'The Architectural Remembrancer: being a collection of New and Useful Designs of Ornamented Buildings and Decorations to which are added a variety of chimney-pieces . . . the whole . . . engraved on fifty copper plates', 1751. 'An Essay in Defence of Ancient Architecture or, a Parallel of the Ancient Buildings with the Modern; . . .' 1728.

JOSEPH MOXON
'Vignola; or the Compleat Architect Shewing in a Plain and Easie way the Rules of the Five Orders of Architecture', 1655. 'The Theory and Practice of Architecture: or Vitruvius and Vignola abridg'd. The first by . . . Mr Perrault . . . and carefully done into English. And the other by J. Moxon and now accurately publish'd the fifth time', 1703.

RICHARD NEVE
'The City and Country Purchaser and Builder's Dictionary; or the Compleat Builders Guide', 1703.

WILLIAM PAIN
'The Builder's Pocket-Treasure; or Palladio delineated and explained', 1763. 'The Builder's Companion . . .' 1769. 'The Practical Builder or Workman's General Assistant . . .', 1774. 'The Builder's Companion and Workman's General Assistant', 1762. RIBA Library.

THOMAS RAWLINS
'Familiar Architecture; consisting of original Designs of Houses for Gentlemen and Tradesmen; Parsonages; Summer Retreats; Banqueting Rooms; and Churches to which is added the masonry of the semi circular and elliptical arches etc.', 1768.

WILLIAM SALMON
'Palladio Londinensis: or, the London Art of Building', 1734.

ABRAHAM SWAN
'A Collection of Designs in Architecture: to which are added . . . Designs of Stone and Timber bridges, 2 vols.', 1757.

ISAAC WARE
'A Complete Body of Architecture adorned, with plans and elevations from original designs . . . in which are interspersed some designs of Inigo Jones, never before published'. 1735. 'Designs of Inigo Jones and others published by Isaac Ware', 1735.

SIR HENRY WOTTON
'The Grounde-rules of Architecture collected from the Best Authors and Examples'. 1686.